RUNNING ON EMPTY NO MORE

Praises for *Running on Empty No More*

Jonice Webb opens doors to richer, more connected relationships by naming the elephant in the room "Childhood Emotional Neglect" and offering readers clear guidance and support to talk with their loved ones on a new and deeper level. This book will speak to many."
—Harville Hendrix, Ph. D. and Helen LaKelly Hunt, Ph. D.,
authors of *Getting the Love You Want: A Guide for Couples and The Space Between: The Point of Connection*

Filled with examples of well-meaning people struggling in their relationships, Jonice Webb not only illustrates what's missing between adults and their parents, husbands and their wives, and parents and their children; she also explains exactly what to do about it.
—Terry Real, internationally recognized family therapist, speaker and author, *Good Morning America, The Today Show, 20/20, Oprah* and *The New York Times*

Dr. Jonice Webb describes the almost indescribable in a way you can understand. Childhood emotional neglect can cause trauma and long-lasting devastating effects on emotional development and relationships. Embrace it now. In Dr. Webb's book, Running on Empty No More, you will find practical solutions for everyday life to heal yourself and your relationships. This is a terrific new resource that I will be recommending to many clients now and in the future!
—Dr. Karyl McBride, author of *Will I Ever Be Good Enough? Healing the Daughters of Narcissistic Mothers* and *Will I Ever Be Free of You? How to Navigate a High-Conflict Divorce from a Narcissist and Heal Your Family*

In Dr. Jonice Webb's second book, *Running on Empty No More*, she turns the powerful lens of Childhood Emotional Neglect from healing the individual to strengthening and deepening the most important relationships in our lives. She answers questions like:

How can parents change their interactions with their children to provide them with the emotional validation they need in order to grow into healthy, strong adults? Can relationships with emotionally neglectful parents be healed? How do you reach out to an emotionally neglectful partner or spouse? By combining riveting, personal vignettes with clear, practical exercises and touches of humor, *Running on Empty No More* answers all of these questions in a way that will validate and motivate readers.

—**Randi Kreger,** nationally recognized speaker and expert on borderline personality disorder and author of the international bestsellers, *Stop Walking on Eggshells* and *The Essential Family Guide to Borderline Personality Disorder. Founder of BPDcentral.com*

Jonice Webb has hit another home run with her book, *Running on Empty No More*. A well-organized and comprehensive book about the practical side of Childhood Emotional Neglect (CEN), Dr. Webb's work is especially poignant because the material is fresh and relevant, the explanations are clearly articulated, and her writing style is refreshingly down-to-earth and accessible. Clinicians like myself as well as the lay reader will find this book to be a necessary companion to her break-through bestseller, *Running on Empty*, which introduced a topic that needed to see the light of day. As an amorphous but wide-spread condition, readers of her first book will applaud Dr. Webb's use of illustrative case examples, step by step instructions, practical exercises and skill building worksheets. I will be recommending this book to my clients, and to those who want to understand that CEN is not curse, but a legitimate psychological condition which a person can overcome.

—**Ross Rosenberg, M.Ed., LCPC, CADC**, author of *The Human Magnet Syndrome: Why We Love People Who Hurt Us*

Dr. Webb's first book, *Running on Empty*, was a paradigm-changer. In *Running on Empty No More*, which is helpful for laypeople and clinicians alike, she expands on the idea of Childhood Emotional Neglect and provides readers with concrete ways to change their interactions with the people most important to them. Written in easy-to-understand but descriptive language, with lots of examples, Dr. Webb helps readers learn how to create healthier, more expressive, and more fulfilling relationships with the central people in their lives.

—**Samantha Rodman, PhD, LLC**, Founder of Drpsychmom.com and author of *52 Emails to Transform Your Marriage* and *How to Talk to Your Kids About Your Divorce*.

RUNNING ON EMPTY NO MORE

*Transform Your Relationships
With Your Partner,
Your Parents and Your Children*

Jonice Webb, PhD

NEW YORK

LONDON • NASHVILLE • MELBOURNE • VANCOUVER

RUNNING ON EMPTY NO MORE

Transform Your Relationships With Your Partner,
Your Parents and Your Children

Published in New York, New York, by Morgan James Publishing. Morgan James is a trademark of Morgan James, LLC. www.MorganJamesPublishing.com

The Morgan James Speakers Group can bring authors to your live event. For more information or to book an event visit The Morgan James Speakers Group at www.TheMorganJamesSpeakersGroup.com.

ISBN 978-1-68350-673-7 paperback
ISBN 978-1-68350-674-4 eBook
Library of Congress Control Number: 2017911451

Cover Design by:
Rachel Lopez
www.r2cdesign.com

Interior Design by:
Bonnie Bushman
The Whole Caboodle Graphic Design

Author photo by:
Sue Bruce Photography

In an effort to support local communities, raise awareness and funds, Morgan James Publishing donates a percentage of all book sales for the life of each book to Habitat for Humanity Peninsula and Greater Williamsburg.

Get involved today! Visit
www.MorganJamesBuilds.com

For My Clients

TABLE OF CONTENTS

ACKNOWLEDGMENTS

Asking for help is not my forte, to put it mildly. But certain people in my life are so supportive of me, and by extension my work, that asking them to read my manuscript, to give me feedback on it, or to fix a technical issue is easy. With these few people, asking for help doesn't even feel like asking for help.

Denise Waldron, herself an author and in the process of writing her own book, always manages to read my chapters, correct errors for me big and small, and deliver honest reactions. I can never thank Denise enough for being a supportive, honest, reliable colleague and trusted friend.

Mike Feinstein, another forthright and trusted friend, squeezed his reading and review of the manuscript of this book into train rides on a business trip, and delivered incredibly helpful observations and honest reactions to the material in record time, just as I needed it.

My dear husband Seth was always there for multiple emergencies like when I needed technical help with the creation of Change Sheets, decision-making input, or a pep talk. Seth, I can't imagine how I could possibly have written this book without your constant supportive presence and unquestioning, unshakable belief in my ability to write and deliver.

No doubt, this book is far better because of the multiple bright minds that contributed questions, observations, reactions, criticisms and suggestions.

Danielle DeTora, PsyD, read and responded to this book as a psychologist, and through her careful assessment of each section, helped me make this book much stronger.

Joyce Davis, LICSW not only read for me, but also, with her therapist hat on, gave me suggestions as needed to improve the manuscript. Joanie Schaffner, LICSW offered crucial objective advice on one section.

Many thanks to my agent Michael Ebeling, who was the one to say, "It's time for you to write another book," and then helped me figure out the best way to do it. And to Tabitha Moore, who has helped me reach so many more people with my message than I could ever have done on my own.

Two major inspirations for this book, as well as the prior one, are my children, Lydia and Isaac. Raising you has required me to ask questions I would never have otherwise known to ask, and grow in ways that I would never have otherwise known were possible. Just by being who you are, you taught me what really matters in this world. If not for you, this book could never have been imagined.

Lastly, I would like to thank my dad, now 15 years gone. In your final days, you said seven words to me that planted the first seeds of my realization of the power of Childhood Emotional Neglect. I have included your words in this book, in hopes that they may inspire others, as they did me.

INTRODUCTION

In 2012 I wrote *Running on Empty: Overcome Your Childhood Emotional Neglect*. Since the day of its publication, I have received thousands of messages from readers who are relieved to finally understand what's been weighing on them for their entire lives.

Some of these folks have had epiphanies that turned their lives around by dramatically alleviating their shame and confusion, and setting them on a forward path. For others it's been more of a series of quiet realizations taking them out of the darkness and into the light of self-understanding and strength.

Beginning to feel your emotions is no small thing. In fact, it's deceptively tremendous. As you chip away the wall that your child self built to block out your emotions, you begin to feel more and more valid, and more and more alive.

If you started out feeling little to nothing, you can find yourself a bit disconcerted by these new experiences. Bit by bit, you find yourself feeling the weight of sadness in your chest, the zing of excitement in your belly, or perhaps some anger or hurt from past wrongs that were done you. Some of these emotions can be painful, yes. Others are joyous and loving. All of them, positive and negative, connect you to your true self, to the world, and to the people around you in a new way that you never imagined.

Everyone is different, of course. But one factor is shared by all who are on the path of CEN Recovery: all are changing their lives by changing themselves on the inside. And changing on the inside has ripple effects on the outside. Every positive, healthy change that you make in yourself affects the people around you. This can lead to some very unexpected challenges.

And that is the reason for this book.

Before we go on, a quick refresher on Childhood Emotional Neglect (or CEN). CEN is as simple in its definition as it is devastating in its effects.

Childhood Emotional Neglect is what happens when, throughout your childhood, your parents fail to respond *enough* to your emotional needs.

What happens to you as a child, growing up in a household that is either blind to your emotions or intolerant of what you feel? You must adapt to your situation. To ensure that you don't burden your parents with your feelings or emotional needs, you push your emotions down and away. You become intolerant of your own feelings, and you try hard to have no needs.

Most likely all of this happens outside of your conscious awareness. Your little child brain knows exactly what to do to protect you, and how to do it. A metaphorical wall is constructed to block your feelings away, protecting your parents from needing to deal with them. This automatic, adaptive move may serve you quite well in your childhood home, but as an adult, you will suffer.

Living life with your own feelings partially walled off is painful and challenging. Your emotions, which should be connecting you, motivating you, stimulating and guiding you, are not available enough to do their job. You find yourself living in a world that seems less bright, less vivid, and less interesting than the world you see others enjoying. You struggle to know what you want, what you need, or how to thrive. Indeed, you find yourself running on empty.

These natural effects of having your emotions walled off can also be quite baffling. Especially if your parents provided for you well materially, or if they loved you and did their best while raising you, you will struggle to understand why you're not happier, and why you feel different from others in some unnamable way. "What am I missing that others seem to have? What is wrong with me?"

The reality is that what you are missing is the most vital thing you need in order to have rewarding, resilient, meaningful relationships. You are missing ready access to your emotions. A CEN relationship can often be described as a watered-down version of what a relationship should be. Sadly, most CEN couples don't realize this, since it's all they have ever known.

Wondering if you have CEN?

CEN can be invisible and hard to remember, so it can be difficult to know if you have it. If what you have read so far rings true to you, I invite you to visit drjonicewebb.com/cen-questionnaire and take the Emotional Neglect Questionnaire.

To learn how the CEN adaptive pattern in childhood continues to affect you throughout your adult years and how to heal it, see my first book, *Running on Empty: Overcome Your Childhood Emotional Neglect.*

If you've already realized that CEN is a part of your life and are experiencing some of the benefits of addressing it, or if you suspect that someone you care about has CEN, read on. Because this book is for you.

Recovery from CEN is a process. As you recover, you start to feel differently and act differently. As you get in touch with your feelings, you have more energy, more motivation and more direction. As you get to know yourself better, you realize that you have wishes and needs, and what those wishes and needs are. As you realize that you're not weak or damaged after all, you start feeling good about taking up more space. You start to realize that you are just as valid and important as everyone else. You start feeling closer to the people around you, and you may start wanting more emotional substance back from them.

As you're working hard, cleaning up all of the havoc that CEN has wreaked throughout the decades of your life, you can't help but wreak more havoc of a different kind. It's a healthy kind of havoc that's brought on by the healthy changes you are making. Yet it's havoc nonetheless.

The transformation of the CEN person may be dramatic, may be slow and steady, may be intermittent/sporadic, or may be all three at different times. But no matter how you transform your inner self, it affects the people who are closest to you. They may become puzzled, confused or surprised by you. They may sense different feelings, or a different depth of feelings coming from you. They may find you more assertive, and they may even resent you for it.

No matter where you are in your recovery, simply becoming aware of your CEN can throw many parts of your life into question. As you see the effects of CEN, you may feel your own relationships disrupted. You may feel angry or guilty or irritated at your parents or your spouse. You may become aware of what you're *not* getting from these people to whom you are the closest. You may become aware of what you've *not* been giving them.

What do you do when you are becoming healthier and changing for the better, and yet you find your life becoming more complex?

The Three Big Questions I Get Most Often:

1. How do I heal the effects of CEN on my relationship?
2. How do I deal with my parents, now that I realize they emotionally neglected me?
3. How do I deal with the effects of CEN that I now see in my children?

Each of these Three Big Questions encompasses many more:

- I think my husband has CEN. How do I talk with him about it?
- What about the special case in which both partners in a relationship grew up with CEN?

- Should I talk with my parents about Emotional Neglect? How do I do it?
- I feel guilty about how angry I am at my parents. What should I do?
- I can see how CEN has affected the way I've raised my children. Is it too late to fix it?
- I can see the effects of CEN on my adult children. How can I reach out to talk with them about CEN?
- Is it possible to heal the emotional distance in my relationship?

If any of these questions resonate with you, you are not alone. You are in the same boat with many other CEN people like yourself who are working and striving to better their lives.

You are brave, and you are strong. Otherwise you would not be reading this. You deserve guidance, warmth and care. You deserve the answers and help that you were denied in childhood.

It is for you that I write this book.

PART 1

CEN AND YOUR RELATIONSHIP

Chapter 1

THE CEN RELATIONSHIP: A PORTRAIT

When One Partner Has CEN

Marcel and May

Driving home from work *alone in his car, Marcel is lost in thought. In his mind he's replaying over and over the scenario that happened the previous night between himself and his wife, May.*

In the scenario, Marcel walked through the door, dropped his briefcase on the floor, crouched down and opened his arms to his two small children, who ran into his arms yelling, "Daddyyyyyy!!" The giant hug turned into a wrestling match as he took turns tickling one after the other.

"Children, get off your dad! He's been working all day and he's too tired for silliness," he heard May declare loudly as she walked into the room. Marcel watched his children's small faces fall a bit as they extricated themselves from the Daddy Pile. His own heart sinking a little, he stood up and gave May a hug.

Distractedly, May gave him a half-hug back while glancing over her shoulder. "Can you fix that broken window this evening? And keep an eye on the kids for a second?" she asked as she ran down the steps into the basement to get something.

Watching the children play, Marcel had an uncomfortable feeling in his gut. Sad, lost, alone. Yes, definitely alone. He mustered his courage to try to talk to May when she came back up those steps.

"May, I need to talk to you for a minute," he said to her that evening after the kids were in bed. "I just keep feeling like something is wrong with us."

"What? What are you talking about? I don't understand," May responded, with tears instantly springing to her eyes. "Do you not love me anymore?"

"Of course I love you, as much as ever," he reassured her. "It's just...I don't know what it is. I just don't really feel like everything is how it should be," Marcel began. As he finished the sentence, he looked up and saw that May's tears were gone. May had seized on the only sentence she needed to hear, "Of course I love you as much as ever..." The rest of his words were lost on her. Already she seemed to be thinking about something else.

"Well, Marcel, honestly. We love each other, and that's what matters, right? I mean, I think you're probably being over-sensitive about something or other. Seriously, I wish you'd just relax and be happy."

Marcel looked at May, fully aware that he had already lost her concern and interest. Helplessly he searched for words to try to explain to her that this was a serious problem, and that he needed her to try to understand.

But feeling frustrated, hurt and angry, no words came.

Fast forward to Marcel driving home in his car the following evening.

"Am I crazy?" he wondered to himself. "Is it me or is it her? She's right that we love each other, but is that really enough? I know there's supposed to be more to a marriage. Why doesn't she feel what's missing the way I do? What can I say to explain this to her? How can I get her to talk to me?"

The portrait above illustrates how it feels for a person without CEN (Marcel) to be married to someone who has it. Only Marcel realizes that something is wrong. He grew up in a world colored by emotion, and now is experiencing his home life in May's CEN style: grayscale.

It's difficult for the partner of a CEN person to understand exactly what the problem is. "Is it me or is it her?" he might wonder often. "Are my expectations unrealistic? Is this simply what it's like to be married? Am I overly needy? Am I nitpicking or making mountains from molehills?" These are all questions that run through the mind of the non-CEN partner.

From May's perspective, everything is fine in the marriage, except for the brief periods when Marcel expresses dissatisfaction. "Why can't you just be happy?" is the typical response of the CEN spouse. May loves Marcel and genuinely wants him to be happy, but she is unequipped with the skills or emotional perceptiveness to understand what he needs or wants. She may view Marcel's healthy emotional requests as needy, or even as weakness on his part.

No matter how compatible May and Marcel are or how much they love each other, their relationship is at risk for growing more troubled over time. Marcel may grow tired of knocking on May's "wall," and angry at what seems like her refusal to allow him in. Feeling more and more alone in the relationship, he may eventually begin to feel hopeless.

Or, in a different possible outcome, May could grow annoyed and smothered by Marcel and his needs. Lacking the emotion skills to put any of these problems into words and work them through, dissent, hurt and pain can accrue through the years on both sides, and slowly erode the couple's positive connection. Eventually, one day they might sadly realize that they no longer like each other very much.

Fortunately there is a bright side to the single-CEN relationship. Marcel knows that there is something missing, so this couple has a huge advantage over many others. May's CEN is not her choice or fault, and Marcel senses this. He can see that May is a good person who is trying, and that she loves him. And everything that is missing in this relationship is possible to attain. All of these factors will play a tremendously important role in their future recovery.

Now let's continue on to a vignette describing a relationship in which both partners grew up with CEN, as they grapple with the invisible issue that they cannot identify or name.

When Both Partners Have CEN

Olive and Oscar

Olive and Oscar sit across the table from each other, quietly having their Sunday morning breakfast.

"Is there any more coffee?" Olive asks absentmindedly while reading the day's news on her laptop. Irritated, Oscar stands up abruptly and walks over to the coffee-maker to check.

"Why does she always ask me? She's so manipulative. She just doesn't want to have to walk over to the coffee-maker herself," he cranks inwardly. Returning to the table with the pot, Oscar fills Olive's cup. Placing the empty carafe on the table with a slight bit of excessive force, Oscar sits back in his chair with a sigh and an angry glance at Olive's still-bowed head.

Olive, sensing something amiss from the placement of the carafe and the sigh, quickly looks up. Seeing Oscar already absorbed in his newspaper, she looks back down at her laptop but has difficulty focusing on her reading.

"I wonder what's going on with Oscar," she muses. "He seems so irritable lately. I wonder if his work stress is coming back. It must be his job pressure getting to him again."

After thinking it through, Olive makes a plan to avoid Oscar for the day in hopes that giving him some alone time will help his mood improve (with the added bonus that she won't have to be around him). Olive makes a plan to ask him about work at dinnertime to see if he is indeed under stress.

Later that evening Olive returns from her errands and finds that Oscar has made dinner for the both of them. Sitting down to eat, Oscar seems to be in a better mood.

After a brief exchange about Olive's errands, she asks, "So how are things at work?"

Looking at Olive quizzically, Oscar answers, "Fine, why do you ask?"

"No reason," Olive replies, relieved to hear him say it was fine. Do you want to watch the next episode of Game of Thrones while we eat?"

The TV goes on and they eat dinner in silence, each absorbed in the show.

The double CEN couple seems much like every other couple in many ways. And yet they are very, very different. This type of relationship is riddled with incorrect assumptions and false readings. And unfortunately neither partner has the communication skills to check with the other to actually find out what he is thinking or feeling, or why she does what she does.

"Then maybe you should just tell me what you want for your birthday instead of saying you don't care."

Since neither partner knows how to talk about the frustrations and conflicts that naturally arise (as they do in every relationship), very little gets addressed and worked out. This is a set-up for passive-aggressive retaliations that eat away at the warmth and caring in the marriage, outside of both partners' awareness. Small, indirect actions like carafe-slamming, avoidance, ignoring and forgetting can become the primary means of coping and communicating in the relationship. None of them are effective.

In the scenario above Oscar misinterprets Olive's thoughtless absorption in her reading as "manipulative," and Olive misinterprets Oscar's irritation with her as the possible result of job stress. Instead of dealing with these issues directly in the moment, Olive chooses avoidance for the day. Her question to Oscar that evening at dinner is too simple and off-target to yield any useful information. She is left with a false sense of reassurance that Oscar's mood magically improved, and that nothing was really wrong in the first place.

So forward they go, into the coming weeks, months and years, with Oscar viewing Olive as lazy and manipulative, and Olive on constant guard against a return of Oscar's job stress. Drastically out of tune with one another, they live in separate worlds, growing ever distant from each other.

Olive and Oscar sometimes feel more alone when they are together than they do when they are apart. They are divided by a chasm as wide as the ocean. They each sense that something important is wrong, but sadly, neither can consciously describe or name it.

Fortunately for Olive and Oscar, they actually have loads of potential. They each have plenty of feelings; they are simply not aware of those feelings or able to use them in a healthy, relationship-enriching way. At the heart of their marriage is companionship, history, concern and love. All that is really missing from their marriage is awareness and skills, both of which can be learned. There is a good chance that one day, one of them will "wake up" emotionally, and knock on the other's wall.

As you read on you will see that is exactly what happened.

Chapter 2

DID CEN AFFECT YOUR CHOICE OF PARTNER?

 It would be so much easier if your empty space would
" *simply sit there, inert. But emptiness does not do so.* "

Many factors influence how we choose our spouses. For example, where we live, our career, interests, hobbies and religion all have a great impact upon who we are likely to meet, thereby determining the pool of potential candidates to choose from.

Your childhood experience plays an important role as well. Childhood Emotional Neglect leaves its footprint on you. That footprint affects every decision you will make in your life, including who you choose to spend your life with.

Five Ways CEN Can Affect Your Choice of Partner

1. You naturally seek out the kind of love you received from your parents in childhood.

A child's first and primary experience of love is in his relationship with his parents. Your parents' own personal style of love becomes internalized by you while they are raising you. Your parents' love, no matter its quality or completeness, fuses with your brain and becomes an integral part of your emotional life (Moore, Kinghorn and Bandy, 2011). The type of love you experience as a child is the type of love that will feel real, comfortable and natural to you as an adult.

Truth be told, this is a major part of the reason why so many people who grow up in dysfunctional homes recreate that same dysfunction in their adult life with their own spouses and children. They seek and find what feels real and comfortable to them, and this perpetuates the cycle of dysfunction that they experienced as children.

When you grow up in a CEN home you may experience love that has all the trimmings: a nice house, nice clothes and a good education, all provided for you. Yet the love you are experiencing lacks emotional substance. This sets you up to experience love that does have emotional substance, if or when you encounter it as an adult, as deeply uncomfortable. It may feel overwhelming, excessive or just plain "wrong." You may actually leave the person who offers you meaningful, substantial love, to seek instead a partner who offers you less, but ironically feels more "right" and more comfortable.

In this way, those with CEN are set up to feel drawn to one another. Those with CEN can offer each other a comfort that *feels* like love, and in many ways *is* love. It's connecting and enduring, yes. But it's also lacking in the quality of emotional depth that keeps it burning, and the emotion skills that keep it strong. So it's a love that can lead to decades of disappointment and bafflement for both partners, just as you saw in the two vignettes above.

Olive and Oscar both grew up in emotionally neglectful homes. When they met, they each felt a sense of safety with the other. Each was able to meet the other's subdued emotional needs, and their emotion skills were well matched. Each would have felt smothered by any partner who required true emotional connection and intimacy (like Marcel).

2. The intense need to fill that empty space inside leads you to commit too soon.

You grew up pushing away your feelings. Now, as an adult, you are living without proper access to your emotions. Your emotions should be infusing you with color and meaning and connection, but they are walled off and unable to connect with you, and that is the empty space inside you.

It would be so much easier if your empty space would simply sit there, inert. But emptiness does not do so. Instead the void inside you is like a vacuum. It pulls for something, or someone, to fill it. You may try to fill your space with food or alcohol, shopping or gambling, work, or a host of other distractions or temporary rewards. Or you may, like many, try to fill it with a relationship. The strong pull of the vacuum may then put you at risk for committing to a partner too early or too soon, or before you know him or her fully.

3. The desperate necessity to never feel or appear needy prevents you from committing at all.

As a child you were not allowed to have certain emotional needs (or perhaps *any* emotional needs). You internalized the message that having needs is weak, wrong or even shameful. As an adult you are desperate to make sure that you never have to appear weak. You take great care to never show emotional vulnerability.

Many wonderful people who grew up with Emotional Neglect are so afraid to feel or expose their own emotional needs to others that they cannot allow themselves to want a partner, or to seek one. Did you start dating later than usual? Do you blanch every time someone asks if there's anyone special in your life? Do you have great difficulty opening up emotionally to anyone you are dating? These can all be signs that you are protecting yourself and others from your own normal, healthy human needs. You are ashamed to have them.

You probably don't even realize it, but emotionally you are Closed For Business.

4. Living in a bland world, you marry someone with intense emotions.

It's true that when you have CEN, you may feel most comfortable partnering with someone whose love is similar to your own, as we discussed in #1. But for some, CEN can have the opposite effect.

As we know, Emotional Neglect can make life feel meaningless and drab. So you may look around and see others living a life that seems richer, brighter and more vivid. All the while your empty space is tugging at you to fill it.

These two forces can act together to draw you toward someone whose light shines bright. Someone who feels things intensely and deeply. When you partner with someone whose emotions are strong, you fill your own life with their power. You experience the emotional brightness that you need in a way that feels less threatening: vicariously through your partner.

Marrying an emotional person may work quite well for some years if your spouse is emotionally healthy, like Marcel in the vignette above. But if you partner with someone whose emotions are excessively intense or unstable for problematic reasons (for example someone who has borderline personality disorder), you may find yourself riding shotgun in a careening car. The problem with living through someone else's emotions is that you cannot be in control of them. (If this sounds like you, see the Resources section at the back of this book for information about *The Essential Family Guide to Borderline Personality Disorder*, by Randi Kreger).

Another problem arises when a person with CEN marries a person with good access to his feelings, even if he is healthy like Marcel. An emotionally connected partner will want and need emotional closeness and emotional intimacy with you. He will feel blocked out, stymied and maybe even bored. He will knock on your wall, trying to reach you, like Marcel did with May. Eventually, he may grow tired of feeling alone.

**Special Note: If you have CEN and are partnered with someone like Marcel, you may be experiencing some of that special brand of CEN guilt right about now. So I'm taking a moment to remind you of two very important facts: (1) It's not your fault that you have CEN. And (2) Now that you know what's wrong, you can heal yourself and, together with your partner, heal your relationship. Your guilt will get in the way. So battle it back, put it aside, and read on.

5. Taking up little space attracts people who take up a lot. You marry a narcissist.

There's nothing quite like the unique bond formed when a CEN person connects up with a narcissist. The attraction is powered by the hand-and-glove fit that only extreme opposites can feel. Psychotherapist Ross Rosenberg, M.Ed., describes how and why oppositely matched but compatible personality types are attracted to each other in his book, *The Human Magnet Syndrome: Why We Love People Who Hurt Us.*

Narcissistic folks also grew up with CEN, but typically experienced emotional, physical or verbal abuse of some kind as well. Often as children they were praised or made to feel special as a reward for having a certain talent, or for behaving a certain way that pleased their parent. They basked in the limelight of a parental love that shone bright when they did what their parents needed, and pretended to be who their parents wanted. This is why narcissistic people can appear larger-than-life. They may take up a lot of physical, emotional or verbal space by seeking "limelight love." Depending on the individual, this might consist of attention or accolades, having things their way, or talking over others.

What better match could a narcissistic person find than someone with CEN? You express few needs, you feel comfortable being invisible, and you take up little space. The attraction can be powerful on both sides, leading to a unity of opposites that has a particular kind of power.

In some ways you may be relatively comfortable living in the shadow of your narcissist. After all, your narcissist will not knock on your wall, because he's not actually interested in you. He won't encourage you to express your needs or opinions more because he doesn't want to hear them. He will happily and freely take-take-take all the warmth and care that you naturally give-give-give him. His emotions will fill the empty space left by your missing ones. His needs will fill the empty space left by your suppressed ones.

For months or even years, all may be well. But over time that feeling of safety will likely start to wear thin. You may begin to feel not only ignored, but also stepped-upon, or even abused. Just as your childhood eroded away your sense of self, your partner now continues the process of disappearing you.

Summary

Whether CEN has affected your choice of partner or not, if it is at work in your life, it is probably affecting your relationship with your significant other. So let's now go forward to talk about how CEN plays out in your marriage or partnership. In the coming chapters of Part 1, we'll talk about what to look for to identify CEN in your relationship, how a CEN relationship feels, how to talk with your partner about CEN, and last but perhaps most importantly: I will walk you through the process of repair and recovery.

Chapter 3

THE EFFECTS OF CEN
ON YOUR RELATIONSHIP

When emotional intimacy is not fully developed in your
❝ *relationship, it can lead to an emptiness and a loneliness that is* **❞**
far more painful than you would feel if you were actually alone.

Think about all of the major pieces that make up your life: your home, your family, your children, your marriage, your community, your work and your finances. Each of these factors helps to determine your quality of life and happiness. Which do you think research has shown to have a significant, consistent effect upon both?

Yes, it's the quality of your long-term relationship (Helliwell and Grover, 2014). In fact, the most significant positive effect has been shown to be for people who say they are married to their best friend.

Whether you are married or not, your primary intimate relationship matters greatly to your overall life satisfaction. Yet it is, of course, one of the most difficult parts of life to navigate.

And no one faces more challenges in this area than those who grew up with CEN.

To have a successful, resilient relationship, it's vital to achieve a high quality of emotional intimacy together. This requires you to have four important abilities. As you read about them below, please think about yourself. Which of the abilities are you best at, and which are your greatest challenges? Take notes if you can, as this will be helpful information when you start actually learning the skills in Chapter 5.

The Four Skill Sets Required for an Emotionally Connected Relationship

1. **Emotional Awareness:** This involves being aware of what you are feeling and what your significant other is feeling. It's being able to observe your own behaviors and your responses to things, and understand the emotions involved. What am I feeling, and why? What is my partner feeling right now? Why did I say what I said? What motivated my partner to do what he did? Being aware of emotions and of how they are linked to actions and choices gives each partner a deeper understanding of himself and his partner. This prevents misreads and misunderstandings. It also makes the resolution of problems easier.

    Beth watches Mark walking toward her with his head slightly lowered. She can tell from his posture that he is sorry. She softens her expression to make it easier for him to apologize.

    Mark notices an edge in Beth's voice. "Are you upset about something?" he asks her.

    Beth realizes that this is the third time Mark has mentioned being frustrated with his mother in the last two days. She asks Mark, "Is something going on between you and your mom? You seem upset with her lately."

    Mark knows that Beth is self-conscious about her weight. So he takes extra care to remind her often how beautiful she is.

    Each of these examples shows Mark and Beth observing each other's feelings, being aware of each other's emotional needs, and responding compassionately. Mark and Beth each show a level of warmth and care that can only be born of emotional awareness.

2. **Emotion Skills:** These skills involve being able to identify what you feel, accept your feelings, tolerate your feelings, manage them, and put them into words. Each of these skills will be talked about in more depth in Chapter 4. Here's an example of Beth's emotion skills at work, as she sorts out how to manage a situation with her boyfriend Mark.

There's a pang in my stomach and a lump in my throat. That means I'm hurt.

Why would I feel hurt? It must be that offhand comment Mark just made. He implied that he thinks I'm vain.

What is this feeling telling me? It's intense enough that it's telling me I need to say something to Mark.

I need to ask him what he meant, and let him know that I am hurt.

This process may seem simple to the casual reader who does not have CEN. But in the situation, Beth uses a myriad of complex emotion skills that she learned at some point in her life. These skills do not come naturally to those who grew up in households which did not have them or teach them.

In this example Beth is aware of her feeling of hurt. She is able to discern why she feels it. She accepts the feeling as valid, and listens to its message. The feeling of "hurt" motivates her to communicate with Mark. This interaction (even if it involves some conflict) will help Mark understand Beth better. It gives him the opportunity to explain, and to be more careful when he talks about Beth in the future.

3. **Communication Skills:** It's vital to be aware of your own and your partner's feelings. Once you have that knowledge, what do you do with it? This is where communication skills enter the picture. How do you tell your partner that she made you angry? How do you let your partner know that you need something from him? The way

you communicate a difficult message is just as important as the message itself.

Mark is hurt and angry because Beth ignored him at a party, even after he asked her to stick with him since he didn't know anyone.

Poor Communication Skills

Passive-Aggressive: *"I'll show her how it feels. I'll ignore her at my work party next week,"* Mark *decides.*

Aggressive: Mark *walks up to Beth during the party and says quietly, but in an enraged tone,* "You are so self-centered! I'm never going to another party with you again."

Sarcastic: *As soon as Beth gets into the car to drive home* Mark *says angrily,* "Well, I hope you had fun at that party, because I sure didn't."

Passive-aggressive actions are actually not so much communication as retaliation. Mark thinks his tit-for-tat approach will teach Beth a lesson, but it will not. Chances are high that Beth will never connect Mark's party behavior to her own. But even if she does, she will resent him for it. Passive-aggression is essentially trying to make a right out of two wrongs, but over time this method simply weighs down the relationship with negativity.

In the aggressive example, Mark communicates in an accusing and attacking way, and his timing to do so is poor. His words, tone and choice to speak his mind during the party all insure that Beth will not want to do anything to fix the problem. Instead, she will feel attacked, hurt, and possibly embarrassed. Mark's needs will unfortunately be even further thwarted.

In the sarcastic example Mark waits until it's too late for Beth to change her behavior. He does not communicate his feelings directly or with care. Sarcasm is like a jab that comes at you from the side. Beth will feel accused and attacked, and her defenses will immediately rise. And once Beth's defenses are up, Mark's message is lost.

There are an infinite number of ways to communicate ineffectively, and we are not able to cover them all here. If you recognize even just a little bit of yourself or your spouse in these examples, you can safely conclude that one or both of you did not learn effective communication skills in your childhood home.

Good Communication Skills

Mark puts his hand on Beth's shoulder at the party and whispers into her ear, "Remember I don't know anyone here. Don't forget to stick with me."

Mark waits until they are driving home and then says, "I thought we were going to stick together at the party tonight, Beth. What happened?"

In the first example Mark communicates perfectly. He expresses his needs to Beth while they are still at the party, which permits her to fix the problem in real time. He does it in a non-blaming way by simply reminding her. In this way he is not only giving her the benefit of the doubt (that she's not purposely ignoring him), he reminds her in a way that will make her want to solve the problem.

In the second example Beth does not have the opportunity to fix the problem at the party. But Mark is still communicating in a non-blaming, non-aggressive way. Asking questions is an excellent way to avoid accusing the other person, and gives your partner a chance to explain herself. It opens the problem up for conversation, as opposed to setting up an automatic angry and defensive clash.

4. **Self-Knowledge:** This is about how well you can read your own responses and feelings, predict your own behavior, and make choices that are right for you. To have an emotionally connected relationship,

knowing yourself deeply and well is even more important than knowing your spouse deeply and well.

Knowing yourself means having the Emotional Awareness described above, plus much more.

What do you want?
What are you passionate about?
<u>What</u> do you like and <u>what</u> do you dislike, and why?
<u>Who</u> do you like and <u>who</u> do you dislike, and why?
What are your strengths and weaknesses?
What adjectives would you use to describe yourself?
How do others perceive you?
What activities do you enjoy the most?

When you grow up emotionally neglected, you don't necessarily have the chance to learn these important things about yourself. When your parents don't ask you these questions often enough, when they don't notice you and get to know your deepest child self, they aren't able to reflect back to you who you really are. Then, as an adult, you may be extremely flexible and undemanding, but you may not have answers to some questions like the ones above when you need them.

In relationships, knowing yourself deeply and well is a requirement. Knowing the answers to questions like the ones above allows you to hold up your end of your relationship. Your partner needs to be able to rely on you to represent yourself clearly, openly and fairly. It's the only way he or she can make you happy.

If your partner asks you, "What do you want to do tonight? Which color couch do you like best? How should we handle this situation? What's your opinion? What's your preference?" he needs you to give him a clear answer as often as you can. Otherwise, he will be left to make the choice he prefers, or worse, will try to read your mind, which is the very least effective means of communication. Over time it's highly likely that both strategies will sow seeds of resentment and distance. Both will lead to trouble.

Conclusion

Childhood is the training ground for all four of the skill sets we just read about. When you see your parents communicating effectively, and when they communicate effectively with you, you naturally absorb the skills.

When your parents are aware of their own emotions and yours, you learn how to know when you're feeling something, and what it means.

When your parents know how to identify, tolerate, listen to, use and express their emotions, you learn all of those skills, simply by being around them.

When your parents see your true nature, respond to the real you, and reflect back to you what they see—your strengths, weaknesses, qualities, preferences and predilections, likes and dislikes, talents and sensitivities—you learn all of these things about yourself.

When it all goes well in childhood, you are launched into adulthood with the foundation for an emotionally connected, resilient intimate relationship.

Unfortunately for many, not enough of this training occurs in childhood. Did your parents have the skills? If not, they weren't able to give you what they didn't have.

Then what happens? You grow up. You fall in love. You get married, and you're happy for a while.

Then the problems begin.

How to Know If Your Relationship Is Affected by CEN

As you know, CEN is invisible, and the huge majority of people who have it are completely unaware. That means that legions of relationships are weighed down by this unseen force. So how do you know if CEN is at work in your relationship?

If you or your partner has already done some CEN work, then you already know that your relationship is affected. When one partner is out of touch with his or her emotions, meaning he or she lacks emotional awareness and emotion skills, there is no way for the relationship to continue unaffected.

Even if you know that CEN has affected your relationship, it's important to know the specific effects. On the other hand if you're reading this book because you suspect your partner has CEN, then it might help to know some signs to look for.

Here are the markers I use to spot CEN when I meet a couple for the first time for therapy. These are the main ways that it often plays out over time or can be observed in a given moment. As you read through the markers, think about whether each item is true of you, your partner, or both.

The Main Markers of CEN in a Relationship

Conflict Avoidance
Conflict avoidance is essentially an unwillingness to clash or fight, and is one of the most classic signs of CEN in a couple. It's also one of the most damaging.

Believe it or not, fighting is healthy in a relationship. There is no way for two people to closely intertwine their lives for decades without facing some important differences of opinion hundreds, or more likely thousands, of times.

Conflict avoidance has the power to severely undermine a relationship. Not only are you and your partner unable to solve problems by avoiding them; in addition, the anger, frustration and hurt from unsolved issues goes underground and festers and grows, eating away at the warmth and love that you should be enjoying with each other.

Look For:
- You try not to bring up hurtful topics or issues that you're angry about.

- You are so uncomfortable with clashes or arguments that you sweep problems under the rug instead of talking about them.
- Bringing up something negative feels like unnecessarily opening Pandora's Box.
- You or your spouse uses the silent treatment when unhappy or angry.

Feeling Lonely or Empty in the Relationship

Being in a long-term committed relationship is supposed to prevent loneliness. Indeed, when a relationship is going well, there is a comfort that comes from knowing that someone always has your back. You are not facing the world alone. You are not one, you are two.

But it's entirely possible to feel deeply lonely, even when you are surrounded with people. And when emotional intimacy is not fully developed in your relationship, it can lead to an emptiness and a loneliness that is far more painful than you would feel if you were actually alone.

Look For:
- Even when you're with your spouse, you sometimes feel a deep sense that you are all alone.
- You lack the feeling that you and your spouse are, or that you work together as, a team.

Conversation Is Mostly about Surface Topics

Every couple must talk about something. Emotionally connected couples discuss their feelings and emotional needs with relative ease. Not so with the emotionally neglected. When you have CEN, you stick with "safe" topics. Current events, logistics or the children, for example. You can plan together. You can talk about the kids. You can talk about what's happening, but not about what you're feeling. You seldom discuss anything that has depth or emotion involved. And when you do, it may feel awkward or difficult, and the words may be few.

A willingness to open up, to explore problems and to have an exchange about feelings, motivations, needs and problems is essential to the health of a relationship.

Look For:

- Talking about a topic that involves emotion is a huge struggle for one or both of you. Emotional intimacy requires vulnerability on both sides. When you have no choice but to talk about something emotional, it's a challenge of epic proportions. Trying to put feelings into words seems impossible. You typically, as a couple, end up blowing up and/or abandoning the topic altogether.
- It's difficult to find things to talk about. You go out to dinner for your anniversary, and you expect it to feel warm and romantic.

GREGORY

"Fresh-ground pepper? Counselling?"

But instead the table between you feels like a barrier that divides you. In general, conversation can feel stilted or awkward, especially when it "should" be the opposite.

- One or both of you have a limited vocabulary of emotion words.

Emotional Intimacy Is Lacking

Few couples know the term "emotional intimacy," what it means and how to cultivate it. Yet emotional intimacy is the glue that holds a relationship together and the spice that keeps it interesting. It's essential, but it's also hard to tell whether you have it or not. It's also the biggest relationship challenge of all for those who grew up with Emotional Neglect. How do you know if your relationship lacks this very important ingredient?

Look For:

- You are uncomfortable showing emotion in each other's presence. When you're feeling sad, angry, anxious or upset, or hurt, lost, vulnerable or overwhelmed, you try to hide it from your partner. Maybe you don't want to burden her, or perhaps you don't want to appear weak. Maybe you prefer to keep things positive.
- You are often surprised by how poorly your partner seems to understand or know you. You've been together long enough that you should be able to predict each other's actions and decisions. Yet your partner frequently misinterprets what you mean, or incorrectly predicts what you will do.
- One or both of you frequently misreads or misrepresents what he is feeling; for example, he insists, "I'm not angry," when he is clearly, visibly angry.
- One partner claims to be perfectly happy, even when the other expresses deep dissatisfaction in the relationship. (When a couple is emotionally connected, one cannot be happy with the relationship unless the other is also happy.)
- It feels like something important is missing, even though you like and love your partner. Holding back your feelings in any

of the ways described above leads to an absence of the very stuff that makes a relationship rich and meaningful. It's hard to put it into words, but something key is missing, and some part of you knows it.

- You are living very separate lives, even though you like and love each other. You are two planets revolving around each other, and only sometimes do your orbits meet. Lack of teamwork and lack of connection leaves you each pursuing paths that work for you, regardless of whether those paths bring you together or not.

Lack of Passion

If you've been together a long time, I know what you're thinking: "Come on now, Dr. Webb. What long-married couple has passion?"

My answer is: PLENTY. Passion changes over the years, for sure. But in an emotionally connected relationship, it does not go away. It simply mellows and becomes more complex over time. Passion goes from the desperate drive to be constantly together and having sex early in the relationship, to a feeling of comfort knowing that your partner is nearby. You look forward to seeing her after an absence. You have a desire to be physically close, a deep understanding of each other's sexual needs, and a motivation to please each other sexually.

Passion is also most deeply felt during and after a conflict. Conflicts stir intense feelings, a form of passion. And working through them together fosters a feeling of trust and connection that also is passion.

Many couples don't know that they can and should have passion, or what to look for to answer whether they have it or not. Here are some signs that can tell you that it's lacking in your relationship.

Look For:
- Very little fighting takes place in the relationship
- Lack of physical affection on a casual or daily basis

- Inadequate sex and/or desire for sex
- Lack of need or desire to see each other

The Chasm That Forms in the CEN Relationship

Marcel and May

In my first appointment with Marcel and May, my heart sank. It was Marcel's idea to come to couples therapy, and May was there essentially under duress. As Marcel poured out his hurt, frustration and helplessness, May sat with a puzzled half-smile on her face.

"May, what do you feel about all that Marcel just said?" I asked her.

May's widening smile clashed with the pain in her eyes. "I don't understand what's wrong with Marcel," she said. "I think he just needs to chill out. I think our marriage is fine."

In Marcel and May's marriage, only Marcel is consciously aware of the chasm between them. Emotionally, he feels a million miles away from May. Each time he tries to reach out and connect with his wife, he finds himself up against a stone wall that he can't get through.

May, on the other hand, has a different experience. Her feelings were not acceptable in her childhood home, and so her emotions are pushed down and away. Unfortunately, the wall that stands between May and her feelings also blocks out Marcel. May might sense an emptiness in her life, but she does not miss what she has never had—emotional intimacy. She is comfortable in the marriage because it recreates the same level of closeness that she had in her childhood. With her own feelings blocked off and with everyone who is important to her at bay, she only becomes uncomfortable in the marriage when Marcel knocks on her wall and demands, "Let me in!"

Each CEN person has developed his own unique system to avoid emotion. Some laugh or crack a joke when faced with another person's emotions; others freeze, talk excessively, fidget, change the subject or leave the room. May uses her smile, as well as the shutting-down mechanism we saw her use earlier when Marcel tried to talk with her about his needs in the relationship.

In the therapy room, May was using her smile to "protect" herself, Marcel and me from her feelings. Her smile is one of the tools she learned and used well in her childhood home. A smile communicates one emotion, "happy," which is the only emotion that's acceptable in many CEN households. A smiling child or adult is not of concern to anyone. A smile does not draw attention or ask for anything. A smile is a way to not only please others, but also to assure the world: "Don't worry about me. I'm okay."

May's smile and her denial of the problem are both effective ways to keep Marcel at bay. She is not consciously choosing either of these methods, of course. They were literally wired into her in childhood, and they are all she knows.

The remarkable thing about CEN is that it's not dramatic. Often there are no explosions or fights, and there's no "bad guy." Couples can have a hard time taking action to solve an invisible, vague, indescribable problem, and it's hard to complain about a partner who is essentially selfless and well-meaning.

One thing is a certainty for every CEN relationship that does not face and heal its CEN. An ever-widening path will take the partners farther and farther apart. Nobody gets their needs met. Nobody is challenged to grow. And nobody wins.

On the flip side, as long as one member of the couple is uncomfortable enough in the marriage to be motivated to challenge the other, the couple's potential for growth is limitless. Warmth, connection, conflict-management skills and emotion skills are all completely learnable. The prognosis for couples like Marcel and May is actually excellent.

Of course not all CEN relationships look like Marcel and May's. Childhood Emotional Neglect in a relationship can take many different forms. The particular personalities of the two partners have great bearing on the unique quality of their CEN bond.

Olive and Oscar

By the time Olive and Oscar came to my office, their marriage was in serious trouble. Years had gone by with little communication, while misinterpretations and false assumptions grew like weeds in an unkempt garden. Each partner sat fairly expressionless on my couch, struggling to explain why they had come to see me.

"I'm pretty much done with this marriage," Olive finally said flatly. "We've been married all these years, and Oscar still doesn't know me at all."

"I do know her, extremely well in fact," Oscar said. "And that's the real reason she's 'done' with our marriage." (Yes, Oscar put sarcastic finger quotes around the word "done.") "She never admits the real reason she does things."

As I listened and observed this exchange in our first session, I was amazed. Interestingly, I was able to tell after only brief interaction with Olive that she was not the manipulator that Oscar described. I also saw the level of anger that Oscar carried, and how oblivious Olive seemed to be to it.

Olive's abrupt announcement in the session that she was done with the marriage is typical of a person with CEN. Lacking the skills to communicate about subtle and varied emotions, and unable to understand or put the myriad of problems into words, she said the only thing she could formulate to communicate the intensity of her feelings in that moment. I have found that many CEN folks are prone to such extreme statements once they finally decide to voice their pain.

Olive and Oscar, in their double CEN marriage, had two walls to contend with. Sadly, in their marriage no one was knocking on anyone's wall. Their chasm had been widening for many years and was now double-wide. They were both intelligent, good-hearted and likable people, and they seemed like they should make a good couple. Despite the misinterpretations and the anger, I could sense love between them.

Olive and Oscar had no opportunity as children to learn that emotional intimacy exists. Neither of them experienced it in their families or saw it between their parents. Both were intelligent, good and caring people, but neither had access to his emotions, and neither had the emotion skills necessary to create and maintain true emotional intimacy with a partner.

There's a particular feeling that I get when I work with a CEN couple. It's similar to the experience of trying to push two magnets together that are facing the wrong directions. It's like there's a powerful force field between them, pushing them apart.

The only way to break the force field is to begin to help each partner to better access his own emotions in some small way. By talking about their feelings and their relationship in more nuanced, emotionally enriched ways, they each make a slight turn, followed by another slight turn, followed by another. Bit by bit, they gradually end up turning their faces enough that a slight pull can begin to form.

And when that happens, the real repair work can begin.

Chapter 4

HOW TO TALK TO YOUR PARTNER ABOUT CEN

> **"** *When you bring up CEN to your partner, it's the opposite of rejection. Instead, it's an invitation to come closer.* **"**

Marcel and May

When Marcel first realized *that he was unhappy in his marriage, it was only the beginning of the problem. As he became more and more unhappy, he gradually realized that he needed to try harder to talk to May about it. He didn't know why, but he sensed a giant wall that he would need to scale to get through to May.*

Weeks went by, months, and then several years. Marcel went back and forth between feeling deeply unhappy in his marriage, and feeling like he must be crazy. After all, there were so many great things about his relationship. He loved his wife deeply, and often enjoyed spending time with her. Their family vacations, Saturday afternoon bike rides, and their quiet evenings after the children were in bed all felt satisfying in very important ways.

May was a kind and loving mother to their children and a successful attorney. Marcel often wondered how he could dare ask for more. Each time he considered speaking with her about his unhappiness, he felt bad and doubted himself. He would remind himself of May's positive traits, and resolve to focus on those instead of this vague feeling of dissatisfaction that dogged him…

Olive and Oscar

After years of marriage, something unexpected happened. Oscar was told by his doctor that he had kidney cancer. As he went through the frightening steps of testing and diagnosis, he felt Olive's presence at his side every step of the way. Strangely, though, he also felt that Olive wasn't there for him. He found himself urgently needing to call his sister Britt after each medical appointment to report what happened, what the doctor said, and the next steps. Somehow, talking with Britt helped him feel better in a way that talking with Olive did not.

Oscar had no idea why talking with Britt helped him so much more. To him, it seemed that Olive was doing all the right things. She gave him constant reassurance that he would be fine, and that everything would be okay. Britt, on the other hand, cried when he told her his diagnosis. During their conversations she shared her feelings with him, and went through the doctor's comments in a realistic way, thinking through the possibilities with him, both positive and negative. She noticed Oscar's tone of voice, and asked him how he felt about various developments. When, after his surgery, Oscar received the news that he was cancer-free and would not need chemo, Britt, not his wife, was the first person he wanted to tell.

Months past the cancer episode, Oscar remained confused by his feelings (because they made no sense to him). Somehow he felt that Olive had let him down when he needed her the most. He felt guilty for feeling this way since she had been by his side through the entire ordeal.

"What is going on here? What has gone wrong? How can I feel this way about Olive, who I know loves me?" he often

wondered. Held back by his guilt and confusion, it would take Oscar some time to finally ask Olive to go to couples counseling with him.

There's nothing quite like finding yourself married to someone with CEN. It's hard to believe your own perception that something is wrong in the relationship. You know that something is missing, but you're not sure what it is. You may like and love your spouse, but you feel distant from him. You want, more than anything, to feel something that you can't quite name. You may appear to be happily married, and in many ways, you are. And yet you feel lost at sea.

There are many possible ways to find yourself needing to talk with your partner about CEN. It may be that you have realized that you have emotionally neglected your spouse. It may be that you suspect that your spouse has CEN, and you'd like to approach him about it. It may be that you have realized that you both likely have CEN, and you want to explore this question with your partner.

Whatever your situation, one thing is definitely true. Since you are the one reading this, the responsibility for taking action falls on your shoulders. You are the one with the awareness of a problem, and so you must be the one to reach out. That may feel like an unfair burden, and I understand! But actually it's less a burden, and more an opportunity. You are now armed with the power of knowledge, and I will help you use that power to change your relationship.

I understand the load you are carrying right now, and how much trepidation you might be feeling about talking with your partner about such an emotionally challenging topic as CEN. So I'm going to give you as much direction and support as possible. We will take this one step at a time.

Our first step will be to get you strong, confident, and ready to tackle this.

Before You Talk with Your Partner

Whether or not you have already tried to talk with your partner about problems in the relationship, it can feel especially scary or risky to bring up this topic, not knowing how your partner will react, or whether you will be successful.

If you grew up emotionally neglected yourself, every fiber of your being might be trying to hold you back from taking action. Your gut might be screaming, "Don't stir up trouble!" or "Don't hurt him!" If your spouse grew up with CEN, you've probably long been receiving the same message from him, either directly or indirectly. Emotional Neglect makes everyone feel like it's wrong to talk about difficult or painful or emotional things. Emotional Neglect makes you afraid to speak your truth out of fear that it might hurt the other person. I have seen many, many CEN people balk at talking with their partners about their frustrations in their relationship, proclaiming "I don't want to be mean."

Please know that nothing can be further from the truth. Not only is being honest with your partner your responsibility, it's also the most loving thing you can do for him. When you bring up CEN to your partner, it's the opposite of rejection. Instead, it's an invitation to come closer. It's vital that you make sure to relentlessly hold onto this fact, and know that you are performing a loving act by speaking your truth in a compassionate way, and challenging your spouse.

Here are some general guidelines to keep in the back (or better yet the front) of your mind as you read the rest of Part 1, and as you start the process of talking with your partner.

Keep These Guidelines in Mind

- It's your responsibility to knock on your partner's wall, but it's up to her to answer it. You do not have control over the outcome.
- Emotional Neglect is silent and invisible, and no one chooses it. So no one is to blame for this problem.
- Your partner is not aware of what's wrong and is not purposely choosing to shut you out.

- Enduring love can, and often does, exist in CEN relationships. Over time, CEN makes the love harder to see, but it is still there.
- It is very possible to heal your relationship from CEN, and Step 1 is both partners becoming aware of it.
- Bringing up a problem in the relationship with your partner is a loving and caring thing to do.

Get Into the Right Mindset

- Know that you are taking a positive, loving step by speaking your truth in a compassionate way. Even if your spouse responds defensively, feels criticized, or gets angry, do not waiver on this basic knowledge, as it will sustain you.
- Manage your expectations. It's important not to expect instant results from one conversation about CEN. Think of your first conversation as planting seeds that we hope will take root and grow into something. You will likely need to have multiple conversations over time. True understanding of CEN usually takes place at different levels, one level at a time. Patience on your part will be a key ingredient to success.
- Be aware of any anger or blame that you might feel at your spouse and make sure it does not enter into the conversation. If you convey even a trace of anger or blame to your partner for her CEN, this will make it much harder for her to accept or absorb your message or give you the response you need.
- Learn as much as you can about CEN before bringing it up to your partner. This will allow you to talk about it knowledgeably and answer any questions she might have. If you've grown up with some amount of CEN yourself, do as much work on your own CEN as possible before you talk with your partner.

Talking about any difficult topic is best done with some amount of planning. Planning offers multiple advantages for maximizing the likelihood of a successful discussion. In this case, planning means purposely choosing the time, place and method to introduce a high-intensity or high-stakes question or topic.

In order to make decisions like this, it helps to know your partner well. Is she defensive? Does she feel criticized every time you bring up a problem? Does he shut down when an emotional topic arises? Will he be at risk of "falling on his sword," or becoming immediately consumed with self-blame and shame for not being a perfect partner; for having let you down? All in all, the better you can predict your partner's reactions and feelings, the better you can plan your talk, and the more successful you can be.

The Visualization Exercise

Research has shown that when you imagine yourself doing something, you are able to perform it better in real life (Sanders and Sadosky, 2008). This works for athletes, surgeons and public speakers alike. Indeed, picturing an action prepares you to do it well. So let's now harness the power of your brain: first to plan your talk with your partner, and then also to carry it through.

To begin, go into a room alone where you will not be disturbed. Close your eyes, and picture yourself sitting with your partner, and talking about something important. Imagine the scene with as much detail as possible. Where are you? What time of day is it? What sort of mood is your partner in?

Now picture yourself saying, "I think that I've figured out something important about our relationship. Can we talk about it?"

Open your eyes now and ask yourself these questions. In your imagination how did you feel when you were saying this to your partner? How did your partner respond? Was the scene the best you could muster? Might there be a better place or time than the one you imagined? If you felt very anxious in the scenario, it will be helpful to re-imagine it over and over again, trying to anticipate every realistic response you might receive, and any aspects of the setting that you could alter to make it better. Remember that no matter how well you set up this conversation, you only have control over your half of it. The rest is up to your partner.

Marcel and May

It's evening, and May and the kids are out. Marcel sits alone in the dark living room. His eyes closed, he's imagining himself driving May home from her 15th high school class reunion the following weekend. He imagines himself taking May's hand in the car and saying, "May, I love you. You know that. I need to talk with you about something I've recently learned about that might explain why I keep feeling like there's something missing in our relationship."

Eyes on the road, Marcel can nevertheless feel May's eyes roll. "Are you really bringing this up again, Marcel? We just had a fun weekend away. Why do you have to spoil it?" But Marcel has prepared himself, and he is not deterred. "I'm sorry, sweetie, and I'm not trying to spoil anything. I'm trying to bring us closer and make us both happier. Will you please hear me out?"

May is silent, and he knows that she is listening.

In this scene, Marcel has chosen the car, when they are alone, and after an enjoyable weekend, to bring up CEN to May. He has introduced it in a thoughtful, non-blaming, and loving way. He did not freeze up or fold when May pushed back. He was prepared, and answered May's frustration with loving persistence. Now let's go back to the scene.

Now that he has May's attention he says, "As I've said before, I often feel like there's something wrong or something missing, even though we love each other so very much. It's been puzzling me for so long. But I think I finally understand what the problem is. And the great thing is that it's not the fault of either of us. And it can be fixed! We can fix it together, as soon as we both understand it."

By this point May, still silent, is fidgeting in her seat. Marcel knows that she is listening, but that she's feeling very vulnerable.

"I'm so glad you're listening, May. I love you even more for that. I recently ran across a website about Childhood Emotional Neglect, and I read about how it can affect a marriage. It sounds exactly like ours."

Notice that Marcel uses very loving words. He is aware of May's fear and vulnerability, and he gives her reassurance when she needs it. Marcel also introduces the concept of CEN as an explanation for what's wrong with the *marriage*, not with *May*. It's very important to never use CEN as an accusation. CEN is not a label, it's a doorway—a doorway to greater closeness and happiness—and it's important to present it to your partner in this way, just as Marcel did in his Visualization Exercise.

Generally it's best to talk with your partner at a time when you are both in a good mood, and feeling as close as possible. You may be concerned that bringing up this potentially painful topic at a time when you are feeling happy and connected as a couple will ruin a good time. And yes, that is a possibility. But it's a small price to pay for the benefit of maximizing your chances of a good outcome.

For some couples, it works best to give your partner a heads-up. Setting up a time to talk about something important may help your partner prepare to deal with something important. Think about your spouse's temperament and personality, and the nature of your interactions. Use the Visualization Exercise to imagine how each possibility might go. Then make your best judgment.

What to Expect: The Elements of a Successful Talk about CEN

First, let's go over your ultimate message to your partner when you talk with him about CEN. Then we'll talk about how to break down your goals to make sure they're realistic and manageable.

Ultimately, your hope is to help your partner recognize these important points:

- That one or both of you grew up with your emotions under-acknowledged (Childhood Emotional Neglect), and that this set up a cascade of problems for your future as a couple.
- That your relationship is lacking some vital ingredients.
- That it's no one's fault.
- That CEN is a problem that is fixable.
- That you both can fill in your emotional gaps and blind spots by beginning to pay attention to, and value, your own feelings.
- That the missing emotion skills can be learned.
- That you love him, that you can have a closer, stronger, more rewarding and enriching relationship by finally addressing your CEN, and that this is what you want.

Your ultimate goal is to get your partner to learn as much about CEN as you know, so that you can have a shared understanding of what's wrong, a shared vocabulary to talk about it, and a common purpose. This will open doors for you to work together to increase your emotional awareness, intimacy and understanding as a couple.

You might recall that I mentioned above the importance of managing your expectations before you talk with your partner. Your goal with your first talk is not to change everything or turn a corner. It's to plant a seed in your partner's mind; it's to get your partner to become just slightly curious, even if that seed of curiosity is buried under some defensiveness. Try your hardest not to expect a tremendous result from your first talk.

If your partner listens, even if only briefly, then you have succeeded. If she hears the phrase "Childhood Emotional Neglect" come out of your mouth, then that is success because you are a step farther than you were when you started.

It's very likely that you'll need to have multiple conversations, so in this first one your goal is simply to introduce the concept. Done. Success. In subsequent conversations, you will work to move things forward, one step at a time. Once you've introduced the concept, your next goal is to encourage your partner to read something about CEN.

Your partner may absorb more from reading since when we read, our defenses are naturally lowered.

What should you ask your partner to read? Here are some suggestions, and only you can decide which to recommend since you know your partner. I suggest that you look at EmotionalNeglect.com, and imagine being your partner as you are reading. Would she see herself in some of the articles or descriptions of CEN? If so, send her a link to it. The ultimate goal is to get her to take the Emotional Neglect Questionnaire.

What to Do If You Both Have CEN

As we know, if you are in this situation, then you have two problems to deal with: First, you have a wide chasm to reach across. And second, you have your own CEN. I know that this task may feel monumentally difficult and somewhat terrifying, but I assure you that it will be worth it.

In fact you do have some advantages over Marcel's situation. Unlike May, your partner has probably not been knocking on your wall, and so he likely feels less rejected, and perhaps less vulnerable in the relationship. Also, you are not trying to tell your partner that she has CEN. You're trying to tell her that you both have it. Your message is, "We have both been living with this together. We are both the problem. We both have to fix ourselves, and then fix our relationship." This language, because it involves you both and not her alone, is less likely to feel blaming, and is less likely to raise your partner's defenses.

Remember Oscar and Olive, the double-CEN couple? After Oscar's surgery, when he realized that he felt a depth of support from his sister that he didn't feel from Olive, Oscar Googled various questions about relationships, and found the term "emotional intimacy." The more he read, the more he realized that he and Olive lacked emotional connection and emotion skills. He began to develop a plan to address it.

Oscar and Olive

Oscar took a step that was highly uncharacteristic of him. He invited Olive to go away for a four-day weekend trip to celebrate their twentieth anniversary. At first Olive seemed surprised and a little bit negative about the idea. But Oscar described the beautiful sunny beaches and tennis courts to Olive, and she agreed to go.

During the weekend, away from the stress of day-to-day life, Oscar and Olive relaxed together. The chasm remained, but they both enjoyed the sense of companionship that had always been their greatest bond.

After two days of relaxation, Oscar worked up his courage with considerable effort. While sitting on the beach digging their toes into the sand Oscar said, "Olive, can I ask you a question? I've noticed that we don't spend as much time together as we used to. On weekends we used to do things together, but for the last year or so you've been making plans with your friends. Which is fine, of course, but I worry sometimes that we're getting too distant from each other."

Notice that Oscar has chosen an ideal moment, and has said nothing that would make Olive feel defensive. He said "we" a lot, and was careful to make no accusations and to lay no blame. He has already anticipated that Olive will give the answer you are about to read, and he is ready for it.

"Don't be silly," Olive answered. "I spend time with my friends because you're usually in the basement working on a project. I'm fine with that. It's all good. Where do you want to go for lunch?"

Here, Olive has given a classic CEN response. She focused on action instead of feeling, she didn't address Oscar's concern but simply nixed it, and then she tried to change the subject.

"Yes, I guess it works out okay. I just miss you, that's all. Do you miss spending time with me?"

"Well, sure I do, but it seems like you're stressed out about work a lot and you need some time alone, so I try to give it to you," Olive answered with a slight edge to her tone of which she was completely unaware.

"Oh, it's interesting that you think that. I'm actually not stressed about work much at all anymore. But I can see how you might think that. I read something recently that explains how couples can grow apart and misunderstand each other over time. I know that I misunderstand you a lot, too. Will you take a look at the book, as a favor for me?"

"Okay, but only if you promise that we can stop talking about this right now," Olive replied. "And you still haven't answered my question of what we're doing for lunch."

You can see from this conversation that no mountains were moved, and no great epiphanies occurred. Yet it was a resounding success. In this brief exchange Oscar has introduced to Olive the idea that something might be wrong and that he might have some answers. And Olive has agreed to do a little reading (Oscar could just as well have used an article about CEN, and for some this might work better since it's considerably shorter and a smaller ask than a book).

In this talk Oscar did not use the phrase "Childhood Emotional Neglect" or CEN. This is because he didn't feel that Olive would identify with the words "Emotional Neglect." If your spouse has ever shared any stories from childhood that conveyed CEN to you, he or she may indeed resonate with the CEN term. In that case it may be a good idea to use the phrase in the first conversation. For some, the term piques interest; for others who are less aware of what they didn't get in childhood, it may be off-putting.

Even without using the term, simply by having this conversation Oscar has planted a healthy seed in his relationship with Olive that over time might grow into a true mutual understanding between them. In fact, by building on this first conversation, Oscar was able to eventually get Olive to the door of my therapy office. We will talk more about that later.

What to Do If You Cannot Reach Your Partner

If your partner has severe CEN, if there is an extreme amount of anger in your relationship (especially if it has built up over time) or if there is a tremendous amount of distance between you, it may be almost impossible to get through to your partner. You may feel that you've made a bit of inroad or progress, like Oscar did above, only to be shot down in your next attempt. This can be disappointing and highly frustrating for a well-meaning partner who is earnestly trying to improve the relationship.

When you find yourself in this situation, it's important to strike a balance between trying to reach your spouse and taking care of your own needs. Remember that there is no formula for this process. Every couple is different, and so every process is different. It's important to pay attention to your feelings as you try to make inroads. It's okay if it's difficult, and it's okay if it's painful at various points. But if you feel it's tearing you down, then pay attention to that and take a break. If it continues, at some point you may have no choice but to give up.

I want to make sure that you don't sacrifice your own emotional health by knocking repeatedly on a wall that fails to open for you. If you grew up with CEN, this may re-create the Emotional Neglect you grew up with and bring back your feelings of being insignificant, shut out and uncared for. If this is happening for you it's very important to be aware of what's happening inside yourself and why, and to make sure that you don't let it go too far.

I have seen people in this situation handle it two different ways with success. I have also seen a few handle it in a third way that is far less successful. In this list, we will start with the option that I least recommend.

3 Options to Cope with Your Unreachable Partner

1.   **Give up, withdraw and settle.** If you have CEN yourself, this will likely be your default tendency. Going back into CEN

mode and living in your own separate worlds can feel safe and comfortable, and definitely easy. The problem is that it doesn't really work. Once you start down the path of realizing the power and destruction caused by CEN, your own as well as your partner's, you can't go backwards. It's like trying to un-bake a cake. So you may be able to continue this for a time, but it will catch up with you and you will, at some point, have to make some decisions.

2. **Focus on yourself and healing your own CEN.** Giving up on trying to reach your partner is not necessarily a bad idea. Sometimes it's necessary to preserve your own health, both emotional and physical, and giving up is your only choice. But you can give up on trying to reach your partner without giving up on yourself, or even your relationship. You can continue your own work: building yourself up, filling your blind spots, learning the emotion skills you missed and opening yourself up to let people in. See a therapist to help and support you, and tell your therapist about your partner's CEN. Hide none of this from your partner but don't flaunt it either. Just quietly, honorably heal yourself. Chances are high that your CEN partner will be thrown off balance by your changes, and it will stir him up. He will begin to feel that he's losing you somehow, and this may make him more open to change himself.

3. **The Ultimatum.** This is a powerful option that requires plenty of strength. It's also the one that's most difficult for most folks who have CEN. Those with CEN tend to assume that ultimatums are mean and wrong. But they are not. An ultimatum, when it's real, is a way to stand up for yourself, protect yourself, declare your worth and challenge your partner, all at the same time. If you reach a point that you feel strong enough, and you are reaching the end point of tolerating your partner's wall, this may be a good choice for you. Tell your partner that she needs to see a couples therapist with you in order to save the relationship.

Tell her that you can no longer continue to live this way. Never give an ultimatum, however, until you are prepared to follow through with it, whichever way it goes. But rest assured that I have seen this option work successfully for many. There is something about facing a potential end that can motivate people to confront their lifelong fears.

For many who are struggling against a partner's wall, some combination of these three options is used. You may follow Option 1 for years, using denial to cope. Then you may begin to really work on yourself, growing and becoming stronger, filling your own blind spots and emotional gaps (especially if you have CEN too). As you get stronger, you may find yourself moving toward The Ultimatum.

This is a perfectly natural progression, and there is one great thing about it. The fact that it's a progression means that you are progressing. So if this is you, congratulations. You are growing and changing and moving forward in your life. If that brings you to a painful point, that's often a natural result of growth. And now that you are stronger, I believe that you can handle it.

Chapter 5

HOW TO REPAIR YOUR CEN RELATIONSHIP

> " *Sharing your feelings about something cuts through facts and details and gets straight to what matters.* "

If you were to take a poll of everyone you know by asking them this question: "What's the most important ingredient for a successful long-term, committed relationship?" my guess is that the overwhelming majority of answers would involve love, companionship or chemistry.

Sure, all of those factors are important. But as I have seen in my many years as a couples therapist, one other factor is seldom acknowledged but even more important than those three.

It's skills!

Yes, skills! Why the exclamation points? Because I'm excited to tell you about skills. I have seen skills stoke love, build companionship and promote and maintain chemistry. I have seen relationships deepened and marriages saved by skills. And now the one very best and most amazing thing about skills. Drum roll, please...

SKILLS CAN BE LEARNED! It's true. Unlike love, companionship or chemistry, you can learn them. "Why haven't I learned them already?" may be your CEN way of blaming yourself right now, and I would like to offer you the very real answer. You didn't grow up in a household that had enough of these skills, so you missed the Emotional Training Course that you were supposed to receive in childhood. It's important to stop questioning and blaming yourself, and turn your attention forward. It is not too late for you. And we are going to learn them.

But before we talk about the specific skills and how to build them, let me remind you of the requirements for a healthy relationship that we talked about in Chapter 3. All of the skill-building exercises we talk about in this chapter will contribute to your abilities in all four of these key categories.

"Since you're always asking, here's a list of my various kinds of sighs, with explanations of what each one means."

- **Self-knowledge** is how well you know yourself in every area and on every level.
- **Emotional awareness** involves your willingness and ability to notice your own feelings and those of your partner.
- **Emotion skills** involve being able to correctly read, understand and respond to your own feelings and your partner's feelings.
- **Communication skills** are your ability to convey your own emotions and emotional needs in a way that your partner can take in, as well as listen to and understand your partner's messages to you.

Now let's move forward to the exercises themselves. These skills are mix-and-match because you are probably already better at some of these than others, depending on the particular blind spots you and your partner have. Consider it a buffet of possibilities, and choose the ones that feel the most helpful. Keep in mind, though, that I've put them in order so that they build on each other, so generally it's best to begin with the earlier ones and move toward the later ones.

Connection-Building Exercises

Increase Your Self-Knowledge

The single best way to increase your self-knowledge is to learn how to practice mindfulness. Mindfulness involves keeping your mind present in the moment, and being aware of what's going on in your body. What are you doing right this moment? What are you feeling right now? Why are you doing this in this moment? Why are you feeling this right now?

Mindfulness does not come naturally to most of us, especially when we grew up with Emotional Neglect. Part of CEN is an excessive focus on the external world. What are other people doing right now? What are other people thinking? And why? This external awareness takes up most of your mental energy, and it takes you away from what really matters: you.

The best way to learn how to be more mindful is to take a class on meditation. Taking a class together as a couple is a great way to learn and bond together. It can be done online or in-person. Listening to a DVD or mp3 of guided meditation offers the possibility of meditating on a theme that is particularly tailored to your own needs. See the Resources section in the back of this book for my recommendation for online guided meditation.

The "Increase Your Self-Knowledge" Exercise

Be sure to start here because, as I mentioned in Chapter 3, knowing yourself well is the only way to be able to represent yourself well so that your partner can respond to the real you.

I recommend that you and your partner each fill out the Self-Knowledge Worksheet. Then, follow up by continuing to add more items. Over a period of one month, pay attention to all of these questions as you go through your day and add everything you think of, both big and small.

After one month, switch sheets with your partner. Each of you go through the other's sheet and add your own observations that your partner missed. Then highlight any of your partner's answers that surprised you. Follow this up with a discussion.

Self-Knowledge Worksheet

What do you want?
What are you passionate about?
What do you like and what do you dislike, and why?
Who do you like and who do you dislike, and why?
What are your strengths and weaknesses?
What adjectives would you use to describe yourself?
How do others perceive you?
What activities do you enjoy the most?

The "I Feel" Exercise

This worksheet encourages you and your partner to use the words "I feel" more often. This is important because these words are powerful. You can argue your point for hours, and accomplish little but mutual frustration. But sharing your feelings about something cuts through facts and details and gets straight to what matters.

Use this worksheet to keep track of the number of times per day that you begin a sentence with "I feel." This doesn't need to be only with your spouse, but do be sure to include your spouse as often as possible, of course. Strive to increase your numbers.

Saying "I Feel" Change Sheet

*Record number of times you say "I feel" per day

	Jan	Feb	March	April	May	June	July	Aug	Sept	Oct	Nov	Dec
1												
2												
3												
4												
5												
6												
7												
8												
9												
10												
11												
12												
13												
14												
15												

The "What My Partner Is Feeling" Exercise

Make a special effort to pay attention to what your partner is feeling throughout the day. This exercise pairs emotional awareness with partner-awareness. In the beginning, do not feel that you have to be right, as no one is ever guaranteed to be right about what someone else is feeling.

Warning: Take care with this exercise, as it can easily be misused, crossing the line to become mind reading. Mind reading is a dangerous and slippery slope that many couples fall into. Paying attention to what your partner is feeling is intended to be a way to make you more attentive to each other's emotions. It is not intended to be used as a substitute for communication. Keep in mind that you are each responsible for putting your own feelings into words for the other.

Trying to imagine what your partner is feeling will increase your emotional attunement as a couple. The goal is to get better at reading your spouse's body language and expressions so that you can respond better. And to get better, it helps to check your perceptions with your partner. While simply paying attention and asking is extremely helpful, it may help if you both use the worksheet to record your "readings" throughout the day, and compare sheets in the evening. So I've created a special **What My Partner Is Feeling Sheet** for you to use.

What My Partner Is Feeling Sheet

*Record what you think your partner is feeling 3 times per day

SUN	Morning	
	Afternoon	
	Evening	
MON	Morning	
	Afternoon	
	Evening	
TUE	Morning	
	Afternoon	
	Evening	
WED	Morning	
	Afternoon	
	Evening	
THU	Morning	
	Afternoon	
	Evening	
FRI	Morning	
	Afternoon	
	Evening	
SAT	Morning	
	Afternoon	
	Evening	

Respond to Your Partner's Feelings

When you're beginning to see progress in your self-awareness and noticing your partner's feelings, it may be time to start trying to respond to his feelings in the moment that you're observing them. This might involve responses like:

> *You look irritated.*
> *Are you upset about what I just said?*
> *Did that hurt your feelings?*
> *You seem to be relaxed right now.*
> *You didn't seem to like that.*
> *I can see how stressed you are.*
> *I know, that was sad, wasn't it.*
> *You look like you need a big bear hug right now. Can I give you one?*

Pay attention to your partner's responses. When you get it right you will achieve emotional attunement, which means that you'll feel a moment of connection with your partner. When you get it wrong, you'll get helpful feedback and corrected information that will help you hone your emotion skills. Responding more to your partner's feelings will also get you and your partner more comfortable communicating on a more emotional level. This is an important building block for emotional intimacy.

Scheduled Communication

This exercise seems very simple, but it can be a challenge for CEN couples. Schedule a specific time slot each day to talk together. Use your own judgment, together with your partner, to decide the length of each slot. You may want to start small, and try to increase the length of the talk as you go forward.

I often give CEN couples this exercise as "homework" in couples therapy. It's great for couples who have drifted apart, or who simply don't talk enough. There are several great ways to build on this exercise to accomplish even more.

One way to build on Scheduled Communication is to practice using "I feel" during it. Another is to discuss your **What My Partner Is Feeling Sheets** to get feedback from each other. Yet another is to practice the Vertical Questioning Technique. In brief, that exercise involves asking your partner questions during a conversation that require her to turn inward and think about her own feelings and motivations. For example, "What are you feeling right now?" "What did you think when that happened?" "Why did you say it that way?" These are questions that require your partner to focus inward, rather than deliver facts.

Conflict Management Exercises

Assertiveness

The single most useful thing you can do to become better at handling conflict in your relationship (and in general) is to learn assertiveness skills. Assertiveness is far more complex than most people think. It's actually using three major skill groups, all at the same time. It's managing your anger, forming words to express your feelings, and expressing them in a way that the other person can take in.

There are some excellent books on assertiveness. Assertiveness classes can also be found at some community education centers, and many therapists can teach them. See the Resources section in the back of this book for my suggestions for books that can teach you assertiveness skills.

Truth With Compassion—4 Steps

Truth with compassion is exactly what it sounds like: speaking your truth to your partner, but with compassion for how he will feel when he hears it. When you have CEN it's easy to believe that you should not share anything that could hurt your partner. But believing this is a recipe for disaster. It's not only your job to challenge your partner to grow;

it's also your job to be honest in a way that increases your emotional understanding of each other. The only way to do this is to be willing to say things that might hurt. Here are the 4 Steps to speak your truth with compassion.

1. **Pause and prepare.** Take time to consider. Your truth must be expressed thoughtfully and carefully, and that takes time.
2. **Identify your feelings.** It's important to know what feelings you have about your truth so that you can tell your partner and also take responsibility for them. Are you angry? Anxious? Stressed?
3. **Put your message into words.** Take your partner's expected feelings and reactions into account. Make sure your words are thoughtful and considerate, but also clear enough to express your message.
4. **Choose your time and place.** Where and when is your partner most likely to be open to what you have to say?

The "Repeat Before Talking" Exercise

This exercise is great for improving a couple's listening and understanding in general, and especially when there is some element of anger or conflict involved in the conversation. It works by ensuring that you each hear each other and understand (which is not the same as agreeing) before responding.

1. One person talks at a time while the other listens quietly. When the first person finishes talking he says, "I'm done."
2. The other person then expresses what she heard and understood him saying, and repeats it until she gets it right.
3. Only when she gets it right can she speak her own response, finishing with "I'm done."
4. The other partner then expresses what he heard her saying until it's correct.

5. Lather, rinse, repeat, until you have each expressed yourself thoroughly. If you are both still upset, take a break. Let it percolate for a while, and come back to this exercise again later.

Portrait of a Couple's CEN Recovery

Olive and Oscar

By the time Olive and Oscar arrived at my office, their relationship had gone from highly disconnected to highly disconnected with periodic clashes. This was because Oscar had begun to express to Olive that something seemed missing in their relationship. He had asked her to do some reading about CEN, and she had reluctantly admitted that there may be something they could do to improve their marriage.

The clashes were actually an artifact of growth. They happened because the realization that they had lived all these years unaware of each other's (and their own) emotions had stirred them each up, and individually they were beginning to have more feelings. They were both feeling a little bit of the anger that they had pushed so far underground for decades. They were both a bit frightened about what this all meant, and where it might lead.

I could immediately see how out of touch both Oscar and Olive were with their own emotions, so I started by asking them each to track their emotions. For several weeks we did what I call an Emotions Training Course. Each brought their recordings from the week (which were quite sparse at first) and shared them. This got them both looking inward more and paying attention to what they were feeling.

*As I mentioned above, in our first session it was clear to me how poorly Oscar knew Olive, and how unaware Olive was of Oscar's anger at her. After they had been tracking their own feelings and were getting better at it, I gave them some new homework. I gave them each a copy of the **What My Partner Is***

Feeling Sheet and asked them to write down their observations for one week. I told them not to discuss their recordings at home, and to bring their sheets back the following week.

For several weeks we spent our meetings reviewing these sheets. I helped them explain to each other when observations were correct or off. This exercise helped them each begin to see the other's emotions more clearly, and it also began to raise some of the many issues and conflicts that had not been openly addressed during their marriage. (This is how I heard the coffee carafe story I shared earlier.)

Along with reviewing the **What My Partner Is Feeling Sheets**, we also began working through those many long-standing issues. When I felt they were ready, I asked them to begin Scheduled Communication. They agreed to have dinner together every evening with no TV, and to talk instead. As a result, they started to share many more experiences from their day and to feel closer. They also began to talk about conflicts more and to have more arguments, which made them quite uncomfortable.

Realizing they needed some skills for managing conflict, I asked them to each read books on assertiveness skills. We talked about Truth With Compassion, and how important it is to share painful feelings and truths with each other. Eventually Oscar was able to tell Olive how he had felt when he went through his cancer treatments, and Olive now had the skills to listen to his feelings and understand what went wrong. In turn, Olive was able to tell Oscar how she had felt for years about his refusal, 15 years prior, to have a third child. Oscar acknowledged that he had not been willing to thoroughly listen to Olive's feelings and needs at the time. So he did it now, 15 years later, and believe it or not, it was not too late to help Olive's past wound heal.

In my office I sat with them as they cried, and sometimes laughed, and finally spoke their honest hearts to each other. Some sessions were filled with painful feelings, and I congratulated them *for sitting through them, tolerating the conflict and anger, and staying with it. I explained that this process was the highest form of love and devotion. Eventually, as they shared their genuine feelings with each other, they realized how very true this was.*

Olive and Oscar ended therapy in a much different place than they had begun it. Their previously empty relationship was no longer a void. Now it was filled with all kinds of color and richness and connection. Finally, they knew themselves. And finally, they knew each other.

Please note that this description of my work with Olive and Oscar is somewhat sanitized and streamlined. The process took two full years of hard work. Olive and Oscar were both very dedicated to treatment, and both quickly understood and fully accepted the principles of CEN. Even so there were many detours and roadblocks in the work when I needed to challenge them to override their natural default systems. I had to make them each do the opposite of what they were taught in childhood. They had to fight against their own gut instincts, and this is a very difficult thing to do.

Fortunately, even though I know how difficult it is, I have seen hundreds of people go through this process successfully, both alone and together. And I also know that if all of these people can do it, so can you.

In addition to your marriage, CEN affects many other parts of your life. Now we're ready to read on, and learn how to deal with your parents, the originators of your CEN.

PART 2

YOUR CEN PARENTS

Chapter 6

THE EMOTIONALLY NEGLECTFUL FAMILY ALL GROWN UP: 3 PORTRAITS

The Well-Meaning-But-Neglected-Themselves Parents (WMBNT)

Oscar

Flash back 15 years in the lives of Oscar and Olive, to long before I met them. Their two young children sit in the back seat. They are driving to Oscar's childhood home to spend the day with his parents. Since both have CEN, neither is consciously aware of the diffuse, empty feeling they are each experiencing as they anticipate the family gathering that lies ahead.

Arriving at the house, greetings are exchanged, along with acknowledgments that it's been over a month since they have seen each other. "My goodness, you kids have already grown!" Oscar's mother exclaims. Later, sitting in the living room while the children run around the house, Oscar's dad intermittently reads the newspaper while his mother makes conversation with the visitors.

Talking over the somewhat loud volume of the football game on the television, Oscar's mom asks them about their drive, the recent weather, and how the children's school year is going. When the conversation lags, Oscar gets out his phone and begins to fiddle with it intermittently as they talk. They move on to the topic of the health of Oscar's parents' long-time neighbors, and then they discuss Oscar's father's high blood pressure.

An hour has passed, and Olive stifles a yawn. Feeling a need for some activity and entertainment, she says to Oscar's mother, "I think I'll go check on the children. Would you like to come with me?" Together, they go into the basement, and Olive is relieved to see that the children are staging a production of Romeo and Juliet. Watching the children and laughing with them, Olive begins to feel herself come back alive from the clouded, bored feeling she was beginning to feel upstairs.

Meanwhile, Oscar sits with his father in the living room. One reads the newspaper, the other watches a football game on TV. Occasionally a few words are exchanged about the game. Glancing at his watch, Oscar feels that diffuse, empty feeling. Without bothering to stifle his extensive yawn he thinks, "Oh geez, we've only been here for 73 minutes. How am I going to get through this day?"

At that very moment, Oscar's father says loudly, "Why did they punt?! That was a dumb move!"

Slightly startled, Oscar snaps irritably, "It makes perfect sense, Dad. Why do you always have to question the coach's decisions?"

Seconds later, Oscar experiences a pang of guilt. "I am such a jerk," he thinks. "I am so lucky to be here with Mom and Dad. They're such good people. What is wrong with me?"

Driving home that evening, Oscar and Olive both sit slightly uncomfortably in the car, feeling a mixture of competing emotions outside of their awareness: love for Oscar's parents, relief that the visit is over, and guilt about feeling relieved. And underlying all

those feelings is that diffuse emptiness that they always feel when
they visit Oscar's parents.

In this vignette, you can see that Oscar's parents are well-meaning. They are kind and welcoming, and generally loving. But the conversation, which on the surface might seem perfectly normal, is somewhat vacuous. As one of my clients once said about the lack of substance in her conversations with her Well-Meaning-But-Neglected-Themselves (WMBNT) parents, "There's just no *there* there." On top of the lack of substance, Oscar's father is only partially paying attention and, not surprising, eventually so is Oscar. (It is natural, and in some ways automatic, for adult children to mimic their parents' behavior, especially when they have grown up with it).

Sometimes CEN can most easily be identified by a bored feeling. Oscar and Olive both feel an underlying sense of boredom throughout the day. That feeling is a result of the lack of emotion and emotional connection in the family. Interactions feel drab, and time drags. The silliness of the children provides a welcome oasis of color and activity that is otherwise lacking.

Notice that both Oscar and Olive felt the implicit sense of emptiness on their way to the parents' house. That uncomfortable feeling was a harbinger of what their walled-off emotional selves knew was coming. If only they knew to pay attention to their feelings, their brains and bodies were trying to warn them of the disappointment and emptiness they were about to experience.

For Oscar, the emptiness alternated with irritation and annoyance as the day went on. Why is Oscar irritated? Why did he snap at his well-meaning father about the game? A part of Oscar's boredom and annoyance revolves around his unconscious frustration from a lifetime of unmet emotional needs. Oscar doesn't know it, but he harbors decades of resentment and anger because his parents have seldom noticed, validated or responded to any of his feelings or emotional needs.

As you will see, it will be both validating and freeing for Oscar when he finally realizes what he has missed out on in his life, and why. And when he decides to talk with his parents about CEN, it will change his relationship with them forever.

The Struggling Parent

Olive

Olive grew up in Queens, NY, the oldest of three children. Her parents divorced when she was eight years old, and her father, an alcoholic, became a bit player in their lives after that. Olive saw him on occasional Saturdays, but generally he was unreliable and uninvolved with his family or children on any consistent basis.

Olive's mother had a difficult time during those years raising three children as a single parent. A kindergarten teacher by day and a bookstore manager on evenings and weekends, she worked hard to keep her children sheltered, clothed and fed. Not surprisingly, for most of Olive's childhood, her mother was simply exhausted.

As the oldest child, at age eight Olive stepped in to take over some of her mother's duties at home. She made lunches for herself and her siblings, did laundry, and heated up frozen dinners when her mother was not home to cook for them.

And now back to the current day. Olive walks into her elderly mother's apartment carrying a covered dish. As she enters, she is already feeling a vague sense of dread and responsibility. She loves her mother and looks forward to seeing her, in a way. Yet she carries an uncomfortable feeling of duty and burden with her each time she goes. And of course, just like her husband was with his parents, she is largely unaware of these feelings or how they affect her.

"Hi Mom, I brought you some chicken cacciatore. Oscar made a double batch last night just so we'd have some extra for you."

"Oh, that's nice," Olive's mother responds. "Please tell him thank you for me." Looking around her mother's apartment, Olive automatically begins to straighten up. Stacking mail into neat piles and putting magazines into a basket next to her mother's recliner, she chats with her mother about Cindy and Cameron, and her mother's health issues.

Suddenly Olive's mother says, "Stop moving everything around. Why do you always have to move everything while you're here?"

Surprised and feeling stung, Olive stops immediately. She had not been aware that she was straightening up. "Oh. I'm sorry, Ma. I didn't even realize I was doing that. Can I put the chicken in the oven for you? Are you hungry?"

In this scenario, neither Olive nor her mother are aware of what is really going on between them. In Olive's childhood, she took over many of her mother's duties out of necessity. Because of this, the natural balance between parent and child has been thrown off. Olive is literally "wired" from childhood to take care of things. She has lived her life unconsciously driven by this deep core feeling of duty, obligation, burden, and a need to care for others.

In Olive's life, as we saw in her relationship with Oscar, she does not consider what she herself feels or needs. Instead, she focuses on the other person. "Is this Oscar's job stress? Should I give him some space? I'll avoid him for the day." (Not surprisingly, this is how Olive helped her mother as a child when her mother seemed overwrought and burdened).

Notice that Olive's mother is generally a well-meaning type. But she herself grew up emotionally neglected, and then she found herself in a very challenging situation in her adult life. Olive's mother has not learned how to deal with her own feelings. So when she sees her daughter moving her belongings around, she has no awareness of her own irritation, of her daughter's kind intentions, or of the reasons underlying any of it. Her snap at her daughter is unfounded, blaming and unnecessarily sharp.

Olive is the last person who should be admonished, but neither she nor her mother realizes this.

So, just like her own mother and millions of other fine, upstanding people, Olive has lived decades of her adult life driven by the core feelings that were built into her when she was growing up. Her internal life is governed by a cycle of feeling that is so deeply familiar that it's become part of her very identity. Duty—Obligation—Burden—Duty—Obligation—Burden—Duty—Obligation—Burden.

As we already know, one day Olive's husband will have the courage and love to challenge her in a way that she least expects. And by trying to give him what he asks for, Olive will discover who she really is, what she really wants, and that it matters.

Then she will have a big decision to make. Should she talk with her mother about it?

The Self-Involved Parent

May

May, Marcel and their two children walk into the beautiful vacation home they are sharing with May's parents for the week. Looking up at the high cathedral ceilings in awe, the kids yell, "Cool! Let's go check out our bedrooms!"

After planting the expected quick kisses on each of her parents' cheeks, May sets down her bags, feeling both relief at having finally arrived after a long trip, and a sense of foreboding about what will happen next. Walking into the kitchen, May hears her mother admonishing the children. "Your shoes are wet! Please take those off. These are natural wood floors." Looking down at her own shoes, May sees that they are also wet. She removes them quietly and sets them aside, hoping that her mother will not notice.

"We got here early, so I went to the grocery store and bought all the food for the week," May's mom states. "I've already planned

the menus. Wednesday night I'm going to make that special hotdog casserole you've always loved."

"Oh, that's nice, Mother, thank you," May forces herself to say. Inside, she is thinking, "Oh, no. What the heck is she thinking? I've hated hotdogs all my life, and I don't want my children eating all those chemicals. My brother is the one who liked it, not me. How am I going to choke that stuff down?"

At that precise moment, May's mother glances her way. "What's that look on your face? I try so hard to make you happy, and sometimes it seems impossible. You've always been difficult to please, even as a child." May feels a jolt of anger that's quickly supplanted by a pang of guilt at her lack of gratefulness and appreciation for all that her mother has done. Knowing, on some deeply unconscious level, that there is no room for her needs or feelings here, May does what she has done her entire life to cope. She pushes it all away, to the other side of her internal wall.

This enables her to say, "Sorry Mother, I'm just tired from the trip. Thanks for finding this beautiful house and doing all the shopping. I think I'd like to go take a little nap now."

While reading this vignette, you may have been thinking, "Who has a mother like that?!" And if you were, I would like to congratulate you on not having a mother like that. It is indeed difficult to imagine a narcissistic parent unless you have experienced one.

Now that you see May's relationship with her mother, you may be able to better understand why she is so very afraid of Marcel's emotions and his healthy emotional needs. Throughout May's childhood, her emotions, and her mother's emotions, were dangerous. Whenever May's feelings were evident, they were sometimes (as in this situation) used against her. And May's mother's emotions and needs typically took precedent over everything else.

So when Marcel knocked on May's wall, trying to forge an emotional connection with her, May didn't experience it as an invitation to connect.

Instead, to May, it felt as if Marcel was inviting her to walk into a minefield with him. DANGER DANGER DANGER, her child brain alerted her. In the marriage, May's wall was protecting her from attack, explosions, accusations and rejection, all of which were her mother's automatic responses to May's expression of healthy feelings and needs throughout her childhood.

This is the wall that Marcel needed to scale in order to reach May, and the reason he needed to give her so much reassurance and love as he approached it.

Chapter 7

HOW CEN AFFECTS YOUR RELATIONSHIP WITH YOUR PARENTS

>   *Built into our human brains from birth is an intense*
>   *need for attention and understanding from our parents.*

Parenting is probably the most complex and demanding job that most of us will ever face. So it stands to reason that once we grow up, our relationship with our parents can be quite complicated.

There has probably never been a set of parents in the whole history of humankind who raised their child perfectly, meeting all her needs exactly so that all would play out in the healthiest possible way. No child is launched into adulthood perfectly prepared.

Now let's talk about the very special case of Childhood Emotional Neglect. In my experience, this type of parent/child relationship is the most mystifying of all. That's because CEN is so very powerful in its effects, and so invisible and unmemorable when it happens. And because it so often runs rampant in households that seem perfectly benign and ordinary.

Please know that your complicated feelings toward your parents actually do make sense, and are there for a reason. And you are not alone with them. Many other fine people are in your boat with you, floating lost in a sea of anger, hurt, deprivation or sadness about their parents one minute, and perhaps coasting through an ocean of love and appreciation the next.

What could be more confusing? It's a recipe for frustration, pain, and perhaps guilt, even *before* you realize that your parents emotionally neglected you. After you see what you didn't get, these feelings all may start to make more sense, but they do not go away. In fact, in many cases, they are intensified.

In Part 2 we will cover the many questions that you have about what to do now. How do you manage your relationship with your parents on the outside, when everything now feels so very different for you on the inside?

> *Should I explain to my parents how they emotionally neglected me?*
> *How do I talk to them about it?*
> *How do I deal with my forever wish to get what my parents can't give me?*
> *How do I deal with my feelings of guilt?*
> *What if my parents refuse to be accountable for the way they neglected me?*
> *How do I protect myself in the relationship since they continue to emotionally neglect me?*
> *How can I forgive my parents?*

Read on, and we will answer all of these questions, and more.

The Three Types of Emotionally Neglectful Parents & How to Identify Them

<u>Type 1: Well-Meaning-But-Neglected-Themselves Parents</u> <u>(WMBNT)</u>

Permissive

Workaholic

Achievement/Perfection

Type 2: Struggling Parents

Special Needs Family Member

Bereaved: Divorced or Widowed

Child as Parent

Depressed

Type 3: Self-Involved Parents

Narcissistic

Authoritarian

Addicted

Sociopathic

As you read on about the three categories, please think about your own parents, and try to discern which category, or elements of each category, best fits them. Keep in mind that the types above are not set in stone. Permissive, Workaholic and Achievement/Perfection Parents are not always well-meaning. For example, it's possible for an Achievement/Perfection Parent to push his child toward high achievement for selfish reasons, not caring ones, and this would move him from Type 1 (Well-Meaning) to 3 (Self-Involved). Don't try to approach this like an exact science. But having said that, getting a general sense of where your parents fall here will become helpful when we reach the planning, self-protection and decision-making steps.

Type 1: Well-Meaning But Neglected Themselves (WMBNT) Parents

Not all Category 1 parents are as benign and vanilla as Oscar's. There are a variety of different ways that WMBNT parents inadvertently neutralize their children's emotions. They can fail to set enough limits or deliver enough consequences (Permissive), they can work long hours, inadvertently viewing material wealth as a form of parental love (Workaholic), or they can overly emphasize their child's accomplishment and success at the cost of his happiness (Achievement/Perfection).

What makes these parents qualify for Well-Meaning Category 1 status? They think that they are doing what's best for their children. They are acting out of love, not out of self-interest. Most are simply raising their children the way they themselves were raised. This is what we human parents do. We follow the "programming" that our parents set up in us, and to change that programming, we must first be aware, and then we must make a conscious choice to do something different than our parents did.

Children of Well-Meaning parents generally grow into adulthood with heavy doses of three things: all the symptoms of CEN, a great deal of confusion about where those symptoms came from, and a wagonload of self-blame. That's because when, as an adult, you look back at your childhood for an explanation for your problems, you often see a benign-looking one. Everything you can remember may seem absolutely normal and fine. You remember what your well-meaning parents gave you, but you cannot recall what your parents failed to give you.

"It must be me. I'm flawed," you decide. You blame yourself for what is not right in your adult life. You may feel guilty for the seemingly irrational anger that you sometimes have at your well-meaning parents. You also struggle with a lack of emotion skills, unless you have taught them to yourself throughout your life, since you had no opportunity to learn them in childhood.

Look For:
- You have love for your parents, and are surprised by the sudden anger you sometimes have toward them.
- You feel confused about your feelings about your parents.
- You feel guilty for being angry at them.
- Being with your parents is boring.
- Your parents don't see or know the real you, as you are today.
- You *know* that your parents love you, but you don't necessarily *feel* it.

Type 2: Struggling Parents

Struggling parents emotionally neglect their child because they are so taken up with coping that there is little time, attention or energy left over to notice what their child is feeling or struggling with. Whether bereaved, hurting, or desperately trying to keep their head above water, these parents would likely parent much more attentively, if only they had the bandwidth to do so.

Children of struggling parents often grow up to be self-sufficient to the extreme. When you are the child of struggling parents, you learn early and well that you must manage for yourself, as well as save those around you who are struggling or in need.

Because you grow up with an excess of adult responsibility, and little validation of your own emotions or your deepest self, you are prone to excessive caretaking of others as an adult, and you may tend to ignore yourself and your own needs. Having grown up this way, you can look back and see how your parents struggled, but this may elevate them to hero status in your head. They worked, they suffered, they tried so hard, through no fault of their own. But even though this may all be true, they still failed to *validate you*. It is extra difficult to hold your "hero-status" parents responsible in your own head for having failed you. So you are at risk for turning your natural anger resulting from your unmet needs upon yourself. You end up prone to self-blame, excessive caretaking of others, and poor care of yourself. You also struggle with a lack of emotion skills, since no one ever taught you.

Look For:
- You have great empathy toward your parents, and a strong wish to help or take care of them.
- You are grateful for all your parents have done for you, and can't understand why you sometimes feel an inexplicable anger toward them.
- You have an excessive focus on taking care of other people's needs, often to your own detriment.
- Your parents are not harsh or emotionally injurious toward you.

Type 3: Self-Involved Parents

This category stands out from the other two for two important reasons. The first: self-involved parents are not necessarily motivated by what is best for their child. They are, instead, motivated by their own needs. The second is that many parents in this category can be quite harsh in ways that do damage to the child on top of the Emotional Neglect.

The narcissistic parent wants his child to help him feel special. The authoritarian parent wants respect, at all costs. The addicted parent may not be selfish at heart, but due to her addiction, is driven by a need for her substance of choice. The sociopathic parent wants only two things: power and control.

Not surprisingly, the Type 3 Self-Involved Parent is the most difficult one for most children to see or accept. No one wants to believe that his own parents did not have his best interests at heart while raising him, but unfortunately it is likely that many did not. According to the Personality Disorders Awareness Network, 6.2% of the population has narcissistic personality disorder, and 1% of population has antisocial personality, which is a version of sociopathy. In addition, the U.S. Dept. of Health and Human Services (2016) reported that over 20 million people in the U.S. struggle with addiction. Even if many of these parents wanted to raise their children right, they faced great obstacles from inside and outside themselves.

Being raised by Self-Involved parents is only easier than the other two categories in one way: typically, you can see that something was (and is) wrong with your parents. You can remember their various mistreatments or harsh or controlling acts, so you may be more understanding of the reasons you have problems in your adult life. You may be less prone to blaming yourself.

Thank goodness for that one small favor, because in other ways, you face plenty of extra challenges. In addition to neglecting yourself emotionally throughout your adult life, you also suffer the effects of having been over-controlled or possibly abused, and perhaps physically neglected as well. You suffer the effects of a lack of emotion skills, you feel selfish for taking care of yourself or trying to set boundaries with your parents, and you may struggle with self-care. On top of that, you may have lots of legitimate anger about your childhood that you're not sure what to do with.

Look For:
- You often feel anxious before seeing your parents.
- You often find yourself hurt when you're with your parents.
- It's not unusual for you to get physically sick right before, during, or after seeing your parents.
- You have significant anger at your parents.
- Your relationship with them feels false, or fake.
- It's hard to predict whether your parents will behave in a loving or rejecting way toward you from one moment to the next.
- Sometimes your parents seem to be playing games with you or manipulating you, or maybe even trying to purposely hurt you.

In Contrast: The Emotionally Healthy Parent

Many people with CEN have asked me what an emotionally healthy parent looks like. You may have thought for years, or even decades, that your parents were these. It's only now, in hindsight, that you are seeing what they didn't give you. So let's talk about how things feel when you are raised by emotionally attentive parents.

One important key point to keep in mind about emotionally attentive parents is that any parent, in almost any situation, can be one. All he needs to do is be raised by one himself. So a parent can be a workaholic, depressed, achievement-focused, bereaved, narcissistic, or have a personality disorder, and still be an emotionally attentive parent. These circumstances are only contributing factors, but many, many parents in compromised situations do manage to see and know their children on a deeply personal level and to meet their emotional needs.

So now, what does an emotionally healthy parent look like? First of all, she pays attention to her child. She generally is aware of what her child is doing. She is reasonably emotionally healthy herself, and has good emotion skills. Since she's able to identify emotions in other people, she's able to identify what her child is feeling. Because she has empathy, she can also feel her child's feelings. This gives her a remarkable ability to put herself in his shoes, imagine being him, and give him what he needs.

The emotionally healthy parent does make mistakes, and does fail her child at times, for sure. But she is there for him, and he feels it. Because of this he never feels the deep sense of aloneness that the emotionally neglected child experiences.

The child of the emotionally healthy parent grows up with emotion skills which allow him to connect with others. He also has a deep sense of support, plenty of self-knowledge, self-compassion, and perhaps most importantly, access to the most valuable resource of all, his own emotions.

Look For:
- You look forward to seeing your parents, and sometimes find yourself feeling good, or even restored, afterward.
- The emotions you feel toward your parents are much like the feelings you have in the rest of your relationships: varied and usually understandable.
- You feel that your parents know and understand you. If this feeling is disrupted occasionally during conflicts, it does return afterward.
- You not only know that your parents love you, you feel that love from them.

What You May Be Feeling in Your Relationship with Your Parents

Built into our human brains from birth is an intense need for attention and understanding from our parents. We do not choose to have this need, and we cannot choose to get rid of it. It is powerful and real, and it drives us throughout our lives. I have noticed that many people with CEN try to downplay this essential requirement by viewing it as a weakness, or by declaring themselves somehow free of it. I fully understand why you may do this. After all, it's very painful to have a deeply personal, human need thwarted throughout your childhood. It's a natural coping strategy to try to minimize that frustrated need or eradicate it altogether.

But the reality is, no one, and I mean NO ONE escapes this need. You can push it down, you can deny it, and you can deceive yourself, but it does not go away. That's why growing up without being seen, known, understood and approved by your parents leaves its mark upon you. But with all that said, growing up thwarted in this way is not a sentence to being damaged. In fact, it is very possible if, instead of disavowing it, *you accept that your need is natural and real,* you can purposely manage it. In this way, you can heal the pain of growing up unseen or misunderstood.

We have already talked about the contradictory feelings that plague the CEN child in his relationship with his parents. Love alternates with anger, appreciation with deprivation, and tenderness with guilt. And none of it makes sense to you.

Do you feel obligated to go to traditional family gatherings, simply because you always have, and because your parents expect it? Would you feel terribly guilty if you decided to do something different that's healthier and better for you? I'm betting there's a good chance your answer to those questions is yes.

However, it's important to realize that guilt is not useful in situations such as these. Guilt is meant to stop us from unnecessarily harming or violating others. It is not meant to stop us from protecting ourselves. You, who are only needing to take care of yourself and stop yourself from being repeatedly hurt or ignored (or both), are the last person who should be experiencing guilt.

The guilt that may pop up and get in your way of making healthy changes must be battled back. So before we move on to decision-making and action-taking, I want to give you some help managing any guilt that may pop up in the process.

The Four-Step Guilt Management Technique

1. **Rate your guilt** intensity from 1-10, with 1 representing barely noticeable guilt, and 10 the maximum amount.

2. **Attribute your guilt** to its true sources. To do this, ask yourself these helpful questions, and write down your answers.

    a. What exactly do I feel guilty about?

    b. What percentage of my guilt is about an action I took or am considering taking, and how much is about a feeling I'm having, like anger, resentment, irritation or repulsion?

    c. Is my guilt giving me a helpful message of any kind?

    d. Is someone (my parents or my spouse, for example) trying to make me feel this guilt?

3. **Make some decisions** based on your guilt rating and attributions. If your guilt is offering you no useful message, try to actively manage it so that it doesn't affect your ability to set limits with your parents. This will be easy if your rating is low. If it's medium, you may need to often pause, remind yourself that this guilt is not useful, and actively put it aside. If it's high, I encourage you to talk with someone about it. You may benefit from the support of a trained professional. I have seen guilt cripple many strong people, holding them back from making necessary changes with their parents.

4. **Use these reminders** to manage your guilt.

    a. Your negative, mixed and painful feelings toward your parents do make sense. You have them for a reason.

    b. You can't choose your feelings.

    c. Feelings themselves are not bad or wrong. Only actions can be judged this way.

    d. No matter how much your parents gave you, it does not erase the damage done by their failure to validate you emotionally.

    e. It's your responsibility to set the limits with your parents that will protect you, your spouse and your children from emotional depletion and damage, even if it feels bad to do so.

Use the 4-Step Guilt Management Technique to stop feeling guilty for your feelings toward your parents, and to prevent your guilt from interfering with the limits and boundaries you need to set with your parents. Instead of feeling guilty, I want you to embrace your feelings, because they are born of your real and true life experience.

Along with accepting your feelings comes a certain freedom that you have not known before in your relationship with your parents. For example, when you stop feeling guilty for being angry at your parents, it frees you up to listen to your anger, hear its message, and manage it accordingly. Is your anger telling you to distance a bit? To protect yourself better? To talk with your parents about CEN? To set limits with your parents? To say "no" to a family obligation? To challenge your parents more when they emotionally neglect you today? All these messages are of great value, and they are lost when guilt intervenes.

To help you deal with your feelings toward your parents, I designed the two special tools below. I hope you will use them often.

Two Tools to Accept and Use Your Feelings

Tool #1: Identify Your Feelings

1. Next time you are to have contact with your parents, prepare yourself. Sit alone in a room with no distraction, close your eyes, and imagine yourself interacting with them. Whether by phone, text or in person, imagine it happening in your mind.

2. Tune inward, and ask yourself what feelings you are having during the imaginary interchange.

3. Use the extensive Feeling Words List (you can access it on my website) to help you put words to the feelings you are having.

4. When you are with your parents, pay attention. Notice what you're feeling, and keep trying to add or fine-tune the feeling words that express the emotions you have with your parents.

Tool #2: Use Your Feelings

To manage your guilt and access and use your feelings better, use the reminders and solutions below.

- Remember that even if you don't understand your feelings toward your parents, they do make sense.
- Make a special effort to accept every emotion on the list that you make using Tool #1. Never judge yourself for having a feeling, and fight off any guilt that tries to creep in.
- Go through your list of your emotions (it's okay if it's just one emotion), and for each emotion, ask yourself: What is this emotion telling me? To do something? To say something? Or is it an old emotion that's based on the past and is no longer helpful?
- If an emotion is telling you to take an action that would likely be healthy for you, consider taking it. If it's an old emotion that no longer applies, try to acknowledge and accept it and apply some healthy self-compassion. This will help you to move on.
- If any of the reminders or solutions feel very complicated or difficult, don't get hung up on it. Talk with a trusted family member, friend, or a therapist for help and support.

Chapter 8

PROTECT YOURSELF: BOUNDARIES AND SELF-CARE

“ *Your parents did give you life, and they raised you. But that does not obligate you to give them carte blanche positive feelings.* ”

Before we discuss whether you should talk with your parents about CEN, we must first spend a little time on you.

All your life you've been living in a paradox. Perhaps you've *believed* that your parents love you, but you haven't *felt* that love. Perhaps you've felt obligated to show care and warmth toward parents whom you didn't feel very much genuine care and warmth for. Perhaps, as an adult, you've always viewed your childhood as good, and now you're realizing that a murky cloud was hanging over you the whole time.

Paradoxes are confusing. They make us doubt ourselves, and they make us feel weak. So in this chapter we will work on getting you in touch with your natural strengths. After all, you cannot change your parents, but you can change yourself. The stronger you are and the better you're able to protect yourself, the more success you will have in making changes in your relationship with them.

In this chapter, we're going to talk about some very important topics. Like how to know when you should start saying "no" or start breaking family rules or expectations, whether you should try to forgive your parents, and managing your forever wish (everyone has it deep down) that your parents could be different.

In today's fast-changing world, one thing has changed very little: the widely held notion that we must always love and respect our parents, no matter what. At first glance, this rule of life seems like a no-brainer. Don't all good people love and respect their parents? Yet the true answer is NO. Your parents did give you life, and they raised you. But that does not obligate you to give them *carte blanche* positive feelings. You didn't ask them to bring you into the world. By making the choice to do so, they took the responsibility upon themselves to raise a healthy child, which is the mandate of all mammals who are contributing to the survival of their species. Your parents and you are not governed by any special rules that require love and affection at all cost to yourself.

This is the reason why it's so very important that you keep yourself and your own needs in the forefront of your mind as you read this chapter and the next. In fact, please keep it there in every interaction with your parents. For if you are sacrificing your own emotional health to meet your parents' needs, you are paying a hefty price, and getting very little in return.

Your relationship with your parents is just like any other enduring relationship between people. It requires *enough* mutual emotional awareness to make both parties feel understood and valued and valid. And cared for in a real and meaningful way. This cannot come only from your side. It absolutely must come from both.

How to Know When to Start Setting Limits

So far, you've likely been trying your hardest to follow the ubiquitous societal directive that says, "Love your parents," and you likely blame yourself each time your feelings didn't measure up. How do you know when it's okay to start breaking with family expectations or traditions? To begin saying, "No, I'm sorry, we won't be able to come over for dinner," for example.

Now I'm going to give you a very easy-to-remember and hugely helpful guideline to follow when making these decisions.

Make the decision based on what it costs you.

"And how do I know how much it costs me?" you might ask. And to that I would say what I always say to you, which is this:

Tune into your feelings. They will inform you.

The answers come from how you feel before you interact with your parents, what you feel when you're with them, and how you feel afterward. In fact, I'm going to put this into a formula for those of you who like math (or even if you don't):

The Positive Feelings You Get + The Negative Feelings You Get
= Your Decision

For example, if you feel physically cared for and like you're a part of a family unit when you see your parents, both positive feelings, but you also feel unimportant and emotionally or personally diminished, which feelings are more pervasive? Which are stronger? Do they cancel each other out to equal zero? If your answer adds up to zero or less, it is your responsibility to take better care of yourself, and to start setting limits or saying "no."

Please remember that you do not choose your feelings, and you can't control your parents. But if you are sacrificing yourself emotionally in your relationship with them, you are paying an unacceptable price, one that your spouse and children, if you have them, are paying right along with you.

May

Approximately one year after the family vacation described earlier (the one with the pristine wood floors and hotdog casserole), May's mother calls to invite her and Marcel and the children to the annual family Thanksgiving dinner. After letting the call go to voicemail, May listens to the message with a feeling of dread.

As it turns out, that family vacation was a turning point in May's relationship with her emotionally neglectful parents. During that trip, May noticed that her children were enjoying the attention and luxury offered to them by her parents. But she also noticed that Marcel developed an intermittent headache while they were there, and that she herself caught a stomach virus. For some reason, the children seemed extra needy of her attention for a full two weeks after they returned home from vacation. May felt down and depleted for a long time after, and was cranky and short-tempered with the children. This experience had made her begin to wonder if there was something toxic going on in her relationship with her parents.

And now back to the Thanksgiving invite one year later. By now, May has been challenged in the marriage in a loving way by Marcel. She has read the entire book about Childhood Emotional Neglect, she understands much of how CEN has been at work in her life, and she and Marcel have made some progress in couples counseling. May has begun the process of tuning in to her own emotions. She does so now, and here is what she comes up with.

I feel:

Wanted + Needed + Dread + Empty +
Sad + Hurt + Angry + Fearful = <0

May's formula reveals a deeply negative result. She realizes that she needs to take better care of herself and Marcel and the children. She realizes that her feelings are telling her to do something that would have previously been unthinkable. She must say no to Thanksgiving.

After consulting with Marcel and developing a plan, May calls her mother back. "Thank you so much for inviting us for Thanksgiving. As it turns out, I think we're going to change things up a little bit this year. We haven't seen Marcel's parents for several months, so we decided to go spend the holiday there. I realize we're breaking tradition, and I'm really sorry about that."

May's narcissistic mother was very angry, and responded by not calling her for weeks in retaliation. This was hard for May, but with the support of Marcel and her own new emotional awareness and understanding, she used the 4-Step Guilt Management Technique to fight off her unnecessary, unhelpful guilt. With this, May did something emotionally heroic. She protected herself, her husband and her children from the toxicity of her own parents.

Oscar

One day, a few months after Oscar and Olive finished their couples therapy with me, they realized that it was time to get together with Oscar's parents again. By this point, the parents were quite elderly. But, of course, their personalities had not changed. Now that Oscar was more self-aware, he no longer blindly set up visits to his parents expecting a good time, only to end up deeply disappointed. By this point he knew that he needed to check in with himself frequently when it came to making plans with his parents.

Before calling his parents, Oscar sat down, turned his attention inward, and asked himself what he was feeling about calling his parents. Here is what he came up with.

I feel:

Loving + Motivated + Interested +
Duty-bound + Empty + Sad = 0

Oscar's Feeling Formula reveals a generally "nothing" result of 0. This means that the mixture of opposing feelings when he sees his parents does not damage him, but it doesn't help him either. I'd like to point out here that a result of 0 is very painfully draining in itself. After all, everyone should feel some positive result, some nurturance and sustenance from a visit with his parents. So, 0 is actually a certain kind of negative.

Based on these results, Oscar realizes that he must take care of himself in making these plans. Yet, he sees that his result is not so negative that he needs to avoid contact altogether. So Oscar makes a plan that involves meeting outside his parents' house. He plans a fun activity for them to do together where there will be some distraction and amusement: a brief visit to a local art museum, followed by lunch in the museum restaurant. He also asks Olive to avoid leaving him alone with his father during the outing, so that he won't have to feel as much of that intense boredom and emptiness that he often feels when he's with his dad.

Oscar's parents approached this unusual outing with their typical superficial and bland acceptance. Oscar and Olive were relieved to have a shorter, more purposeful visit. In this way, they maximized the positive feeling side of the equation, and mitigated the negative. At the end of this visit, Oscar's result had changed from 0 to slightly greater than 0. For him, after a lifetime of zeros, this was a great accomplishment.

Protect Yourself with Self-Care

It's important to remember that for May and Oscar, and more importantly, for you, setting limits and saying no to parents is not only about protecting your feelings. Minimizing your own emotional suffering is key, of course. But there's another, bigger purpose to all of this. When you protect and take care of yourself emotionally, you are accomplishing multiple other goals. You are allowing yourself the room, stability and strength to grow to your fullest potential. And you are filling yourself in a way that will allow you to give priceless emotional sustenance to your spouse and children (we will talk much more about this in Part 3).

If you are to begin to behave differently with your parents in ways like setting limits and boundaries or talking with them about CEN, it helps enormously to first build up your emotional strength. The best way to do this is to put more focus and energy into your own self-care. By focusing on taking better care of yourself, you are doing for yourself what your parents should have done, but couldn't or didn't. In this way, you are re-parenting yourself. If you grew up with your emotions ignored, you work as an adult to pay attention to your own emotions. See the chart below for more examples.

Your Parents Didn't:	So Now You:
Accept your feelings as valid	Accept your feelings as valid
Notice when you needed rest	Make sure you get enough rest
Provide you with structure	Structure yourself
Teach you how to manage your feelings	Learn emotion management
Teach you how to name your emotions	Increase your emotion vocabulary
Model how to express feelings	Practice expressing your feelings
Talk about things	Practice talking about things
Soothe you when you were upset	Soothe yourself when you need it
Get to know you deeply and personally	Work to know yourself deeply
Support and encourage you	Accept support from others
Offer you help when you needed it	Ask for and accept help

I know it probably seems like a tall order to try to fill in the gaps from your childhood like this. And it's true. Giving yourself what you never got takes a good deal of effort and persistence. But one thing helps immensely: it all feels good. It feels enriching and enlivening to finally give yourself what you've been missing.

But if you are feeling a bit frightened to think about setting boundaries, and overwhelmed when you read the lists above, this may be your feelings telling you that you're not quite ready. In which case I suggest taking a break from this, and putting in some work on your own CEN. When you're feeling stronger and ready, come on back here and pick up where you left off.

The Miraculous Protection of Boundaries

Effective boundaries are a key ingredient of self-protection throughout your lifetime. You need them to keep yourself intact through the challenges of relationship disruptions, conflicts, insults and the many challenges to your self-esteem that the world will undoubtedly deliver.

Although your boundaries can help you in every situation, we are going to apply them here very specifically, to your relationship with your parents. First, let's talk about the four different types of boundaries, and how they work.

The Four Types of Boundaries

- **Physical Boundary:** This boundary is the easiest to visualize and understand, simply because it's physical and visible. It refers to the amount of physical distance you keep from your parents. Did you move far away from them? Do you live next door? When you are together with your parents, your physical boundary is temporarily greatly reduced.
- **External Boundary:** This boundary must be strong but flexible. It serves as a filter that protects you from insults and injuries that come from the *outside*; from your parents. When your parents ignore you, fail to notice your needs, or say something inadvertently or purposely hurtful, this boundary kicks in to protect you. It talks you through what your parent said or did to you, and helps you sort out what's real feedback that you should take seriously, and what you should reject.
- **Internal Boundary:** This is the boundary that protects you (and others) from yourself. It serves as a filter between your feelings,

and what you do with them. This boundary helps you sort through your intense anger, hurt and pain, and decide whether, and how, to express it to your parents. It helps you hold some things in, and it helps you purposely choose to let some things out, in a careful and thoughtful way.

- **Temporal Boundary:** We all carry our past experiences of CEN within us, and our emotions do not necessarily obey the laws of time. When your parents emotionally neglect you now as an adult, old and deep feelings from your childhood CEN experiences freely attach themselves to the current situation, and can emerge when we least expect them. This is the reason one small incident today can make you feel pain that seems excessive. A healthy temporal boundary helps you to sort your old pain from the new, so that you can feel and express the amount of pain that truly belongs to today's situation.

Healthy boundaries help you in so very many ways. They can help you move away, or to hold off your hurt and anger to give you time to think. They can help you hold back the sharp retort you want to deliver to your dad, and filter out the old feelings from the new. These skills are immeasurably valuable to help you to develop a healthier relationship toward your parents.

Of the four types of boundaries, the easiest one to understand and use is the physical. That's why many folks choose this boundary first and only, by simply moving away or staying away. Though the physical boundary can be useful, it's rarely a complete solution. It can give you some much-needed distance, but it doesn't help you deal with your emotions. So even if you can move away or if you become adept at walking out or hanging up, you will likely need the other three types of boundaries to also protect you.

Here's an exercise to help you create and strengthen your external, internal and temporal boundaries. First, choose the boundary you want to build. Then follow the steps listed below.

Boundary Building Exercise

1. Close your eyes and count to ten in your head, while breathing deeply and calmly.

2. Imagine yourself surrounded by a circle. You are in the exact center, surrounded by the perfect amount of space that you feel most comfortable with.

3. Turn the circle into a visible boundary. It can be made of anything you like: clear or opaque plastic, bricks, smooth cement, or something else. It can be anything you want, as long as it's strong. If you can, form a picture of this boundary.

4. Although the boundary is strong, you and only you have the power to flex it when you want. You can remove a brick or soften the plastic to allow things inside the wall or outside of the wall whenever you need to. You hold all the power. You are safe.

5. Stay inside the wall for a minute or more. Enjoy the feeling of being in control of your world.

6. Repeat this exercise once a day, and always do this exercise immediately prior to interactions with your parents, and immediately after you see them as well (as needed).

Once you've used your boundary enough, it will begin to operate naturally. But to build it and learn how to use it, you'll need to purposely visualize and practice it. So now, in the beginning, it's important to try to anticipate situations in which you will need, and can practice using, your boundary.

Let's say you're going to visit your parents and you know that, at some point during the visit, your father will make an offhand comment that reveals how poorly he knows you (because he almost always does).

For this challenge, you'll need primarily your external boundary, to filter out your father's comment and disempower it. You may also need your internal boundary, if you want to manage your own response to his comment. You may also need your temporal boundary to help you filter out the old pain from the thousands of times your father has revealed how little he understands you. So right before you go, sit down and follow the above steps to get your temporal, external and internal boundaries firmly in place.

At your parents' house, wait for your dad's comment to come. If it does, immediately imagine your boundaries around you, filtering for you. The filter asks:

What part of this is my fault? What part is about me? Does this say anything about me, or is it all about my father? How much of what I'm feeling right now is from the past, and how much is due to this one comment today? Do I need to respond?

Your external boundary says:

None of this is about you. The fact that your father does not know you is a result of his own limitations, and has nothing to do with your value or worth. 80% of what you're feeling right now is due to old injuries, and only 20% is from today. There is no point in responding. You can talk about it with your friend/spouse/ sibling/therapist later. You visualize your boundary shielding you, surrounding you in a safe, protected circle.

And there you are. You have the power to protect yourself. You retain your self-worth and your self-esteem, you manage your own feelings and response, and you are intact.

Building boundaries in this way may seem impossible to you, but I assure you that I have helped many people through this process, and it is very effective. Don't forget, however, that it's vital to consciously imagine and use your boundaries, as they won't magically appear from reading about them. If it seems too difficult for you, and if you continue to struggle with your feelings and responses in relationship with your parents, I encourage you to get some help with this. Find a trained therapist who can help you build up your strength and your boundaries.

When you have strengthened yourself enough, you will know it. You will feel ready to move on to our next stage. You will feel prepared to consider whether it makes sense to talk with your parents about CEN.

Chapter 9

TALKING WITH YOUR PARENTS ABOUT CEN

> *Now that you've outgrown your parents, you will*
> *need to make some decisions. Should you try to*
> *bring them along on your healthy journey?*

Oscar

Oscar drove toward *his parents' house immersed in thought. He was mulling all that had happened in his life over the last year. He had beaten cancer, and he and Olive were in the process of changing their marriage in a way that was making him feel very lucky. In the silence of his car, he thought about how excited his parents would be when he told them about the 50th anniversary party that he and his sister were planning to throw for them.*

He was feeling more contented now than he had ever been, and somehow it just felt right to share his happiness with his parents.

"What a surprise! We weren't expecting to see you today," Oscar's mom exclaimed as he walked in the door.

"I wanted to surprise you to give you some good news. Can you get Dad for me?" Oscar replied.

As the three sat around the kitchen table, Oscar explained the party plan to them, ending with, "I think 50 years is definitely deserving of a big party, don't you?" Only then, when he paused and looked at his parents, did he notice the lack of excitement in their faces. His mother looked stressed, and his father had a look of actual distaste. Stunned, he waited to hear what they would say.

"Well, sweetie, that's real nice of you to think of us like that, but you know us, we don't like big hullabaloos. Can't you and Olive just come over with your sister, and I'll make you some of those barbecue ribs you all like so much? Wouldn't that be nice, Herb? Don't you think that would be better?" she said, nudging her husband with her elbow.

"Oh yeah, definitely," Herb chimed in. "We don't need any big party. It's nice to see you, son, I'm glad you stopped by. I have to get to the barbershop before it closes," he continued as he stood up, grabbed his jacket off a coat rack, and headed out the door. "Say hi to Olive for me!"

And he was gone.

Oscar looked at his mother, who no longer looked stressed. "How are Olive and the kids doing?" she asked, pulling her classic move: changing the subject.

After reliving the scene multiple times in the car, and continuing to feel worse, a resolution started to form in Oscar's mind.

"They're so afraid of emotion and connection, they can't even celebrate the remarkable achievement of their marriage. I can't live this way any longer. I need to talk with Mom and Dad about Emotional Neglect."

When you reach the crossroads at which Oscar has found himself, it's a sign. A sign that emotionally, you are growing far beyond your parents. Here is a list of all that Oscar had to accomplish to reach this point:

1. He had to begin to see and accept how his well-intentioned parents failed him.
2. He had to stop blaming himself, and to see what went wrong, and how it went wrong.
3. He had to realize the important role of his emotions in his life.
4. He had to realize that his feelings matter, and accept that.
5. He had to realize that his needs matter, and accept that.
6. He had to realize that *he* matters.

So, congratulations, and I truly mean that in the most deep and profound way. Since you are reading this, you have already taken tremendous strides on those six amazing accomplishments. I want you to pause for a moment to see that and own it.

Well done!

Now that you've outgrown your parents, you will need to make some decisions. Should you try to bring them along on your healthy journey? Or are they incapable of accompanying you? Sadly, if they cannot grasp and understand the concept of Emotional Neglect, if they cannot own enough of how they've neglected you, then you may have to leave them behind (emotionally, not necessarily physically).

The paragraph you just read is a loaded one. Did your heart sink as you read it? If so, I understand. It is very frightening to finally face what's at stake when you begin to consider the question:

Should I talk to my parents about how they emotionally neglected me?

And even more scary:

What if it makes things worse?

Growing up without enough emotional validation has set you up with multiple challenges in your life. And now you face a great one. Not all parents can or should be approached with this topic. And not all parents deserve the care that it would require for you to take this risk. In this chapter, I'll help you sort through the implications of the type of parents you have and their capacity for hearing you.

We'll discuss guilty feelings (yours and your parents'), how to use your boundaries, how to approach the conversation, and how to set yourself up for the greatest possible success.

How to Decide If You Should Talk with Your Parents about CEN

I wish I had a dollar for each time someone has asked me if talking with your parents about CEN is a requirement for healing. And I wish I had another dollar for each time I have delivered my answer, always a resounding "NO!"

Your parents may seem so hopeless that it is not worth it. You may decide that approaching your parents about CEN is too risky, too hard or not necessary. It's all okay, I assure you. Because talking with your parents about CEN is a side benefit. What really matters is that you work on healing your own CEN.

If you are not able to talk with your parents, for whatever reason, you'll find at the end of Part 2 a special segment dedicated to helping you move forward on your own.

Yet some folks do decide to do so, and it works. By "works" I mean that it results in forward progress of some kind for the emotionally neglected person. Often, this decision comes down to whether talking with your parents is more likely to work for you, or if it has the capacity to set you back.

There is truly no right or wrong way to decide this. It is a very, very personal decision. To help you decide for yourself, I'm going to ask you a series of questions.

1. Which category of parents do you have?

This question is crucial simply because whether your parents are Type 1, 2 or 3 says quite a lot about how they might respond, and the potential to gain something versus do yourself damage by talking with them.

Generally speaking, Categories 1 (Well-Meaning) and 2 (Struggling) are the most likely ones to yield some kind of benefit, and the Self-Involved Category 3 Parents are a story of their own. As we know, Type 1 parents are not particularly selfish or self-involved. They are not purposely hurtful or withholding toward you. They mean well, but they simply didn't know that they were missing something as they raised you, and they still don't realize that they are missing something now. With these two categories, there is less likelihood of an angry or vindictive response that might hurt you further, but it's important to note that if you do choose to talk with them about CEN, you are likely to stir up some confusion, and perhaps defensiveness, in your parents.

Type 1 Well-Meaning parents are reasonably good bets when it comes to approaching them. They do have a high likelihood of feeling confused in response to the topic of CEN. To them, you may initially seem to be speaking a different language or accusing them of being bad parents. But some may be able to stick with you as you explain that CEN is a multi-generational process, that it's not their fault, and that you give them credit for all the good they did for you as well. The biggest sticking point for the Category 1 parent is being able to understand the deeper, more complex way of thinking about emotion as real, meaningful, and powerful. It may be an entirely new concept to them and they may have great difficulty believing it.

Type 2 Struggling Parents can, in some ways, be the easiest to talk with. They are, after all, probably victims of some sort themselves. Victims of loss, illness, abandonment, or circumstances, they nevertheless managed to raise you. These parents have a clear reason for emotionally neglecting you, and this may be helpful in terms of their defensiveness or self-blame. This means that for Category 2 parents it's crucial to acknowledge their circumstances, the stressors they underwent, and the efforts they made to do right by you if you speak with them about CEN.

Type 3 Parents, the Self-Involved ones, are the most difficult to talk with about CEN. With these parents, there is a far higher risk that they could emotionally strike out at you. These parents have great difficulty with empathy, which they need to have if they are to understand your feelings. Self-involved parents also tend to have problems with accepting responsibility for how they affect others, making it hard for them to own and acknowledge that they may have harmed or failed you in any way. If your parents are these, I urge you to proceed with great caution, weigh out the cost/benefit ratio, and be clear about what you are trying to accomplish before you make any decision to talk with them. In my experience, the most you are likely to get out of a CEN conversation might be a hollow, superficial response. The worst you may receive is rage, hurtful comments, and vengeful behavior. Believe it or not these responses can all be useful to the CEN adult child. It can feel quite healing and freeing to finally put into words your feelings about your parents and present it to them. Whether they take it in or not, at least you have expressed it. At least you've given them an explanation for the future times that you will say "no," or set other types of limits with them. There's no denying that there is great value in that.

2. How much discomfort or pain do you feel in the relationship now?

This seemingly simple question is actually not simple at all. When you grow up with the painful feeling of being overlooked and ignored, it can settle into you and become a part of your existence. You can become so accustomed to the painful feeling that you're not aware of it, and you may assume that everyone feels this way.

To answer this question, it may be helpful to go back to the skills and techniques we learned in Chapter 7. Remember Tool #1, which we used to help you identify your feelings in your relationship with your parents? Try using that tool, but add an emphasis on how severe the negative feelings are. Use the list of feeling words you made in that exercise. Go back through it and rate the intensity of each painful feeling on a scale of

1–10. You will probably be unable to come up with exact answers since this isn't that sort of question. Instead, tune into yourself, and apply the powers of all your new understanding of emotions and how they work to get a general sense of how much pain you feel.

3. Is your pain blocking your recovery?

I have heard many stories of CEN folks moving forward with their healing from CEN *until they visit their parents*. Re-experiencing the source of your problems can indeed pull you backward. It's like nursing a wound until it's healing up nicely, only to fall off your bike, ripping it open again.

Do you find yourself feeling better, only to feel worse when you think about or interact with your parents? Do your parents feel like an obstacle in your recovery? Listen to your gut and be careful not to overthink it. If you feel it is so, then it is so.

4. Do you see capacity in one of your parents to understand CEN?

Perhaps your parents are divorced. Perhaps they are very different from each other. Do you have one parent in the Well-Meaning Category 1 and the other in Self-Involved Category 3, for example? Does one of your parents show more capacity for empathy or compassion than the other? Is one more defensive, while the other tends to be more balanced and open?

You do not need to talk with both of your parents at the same time, or even at all. In many cases, it makes the best sense to choose one parent who shows the most potential, and start there, with an individual conversation.

Think about each of your parents separately, and imagine talking to him or her. Would they hear this best if they were together or if they were separate? When it comes to having a conversation like this, there's no right way to do it. It all comes down to setting yourself up for the best results, and if that means choosing one parent to talk with first, then I encourage you to do so.

5. How will you feel if your parents under-respond?

One of the greatest risks of talking to CEN parents about anything is receiving the classic CEN under-response. When you've experienced this letdown enough times in your life, it's normal to simply stop trying to talk with them about anything. If this is the case for you, it's important to consider how you will feel if it happens with this topic too. (We won't even try to ponder the irony of trying to talk with your parents about how they've failed to respond, only to have them fail to respond.)

Your under-responsive parents might respond with what appears to be some initial concern or interest, only to never bring it up again. They may clearly be unable to understand what you're saying, and show no emotion other than bafflement. They may quickly change the subject, or dissolve into tears, pulling for *you* to comfort *them*.

Imagine how you will feel if any of these responses happen. Will the disappointment be a tremendous letdown, or will you be able to use it as validation of the CEN you grew up with? Will you be able to work with it? Or might it push you backward? Please consider all these possibilities and how you will feel if they happen.

6. How will you feel if your parents respond negatively?

Many parents have the capacity to respond with negativity to the topic of CEN, but especially if they are Type 3 Parents. What if your parents become immediately defensive and attack you? What if they blame you, call you over-sensitive, or otherwise insult you? What if they shut you out or distance themselves from you to either punish you or protect themselves?

At first glance, it may seem that nothing good could possibly come from any of this, but that is actually not true. If your parents are toxic, you may feel some relief from the distance you get. You may also feel proud of yourself for having spoken the truth to them, no matter how negative their response. You may feel a sense of validation in that they have just produced for you the same exact response you would have faced, had you ever asked them for understanding or nurturance as a child.

Think about this carefully, as your answers are deeply personal, and they are your own. Since there is no right or wrong answer, only you can imagine how you will feel, or decide what is right for you.

7. Might sharing this with your parents make it feel easier to set limits with them, regardless of the outcome?

As we have already discussed, protecting yourself from your CEN parents may be required at some point, depending on how much you are pained by them and their capacity (or lack of capacity) to work with you in your healing process. This may involve spending less time with them, turning down invitations from them, calling them less often, or shortening your contacts with them.

In some cases, your fear of being selfish or your anxiety about setting these limits can be reduced by putting into words exactly what you feel has gone wrong between you, and receiving your parents' reaction. At least you can console yourself in knowing that you gave them the opportunity to understand, care and respond. When they don't, the weight of responsibility is clearly on them, freeing you up to do what you need to do to protect yourself.

8. What do you have to gain by talking with your parents? What do you have to lose?

Here we are talking about a cost/benefit ratio. Some CEN conversations are all positive, and some are all negative. But the overwhelming majority carry a layering of some of each. Look through your answers to all the questions above. Your parents' types, their likelihood of hearing you, how you will feel about their response, whether one parent has more capacity than the other, and the intensity of your pain. Let it all percolate in your mind, and then tune into your gut. What do you feel like doing? Does your gut tell you to leave your parents out of your healing, protect yourself, and focus on yourself? Or does it tell you that you want or need to take a risk, and talk? Whichever it says, I encourage you to listen, for I suspect that your gut may know you better than you know yourself.

"When I was your age, I'd mastered repression."

How to Talk with Your Parents

Okay, so your gut is telling you that perhaps you should give this a try. So first, let's get you ready. We've already talked about self-care and boundaries, and I hope you've been working on those. We're almost ready to take all the things we've talked about and everything we've learned, and pull it all together and use it.

Get Your Boundaries in Place

First comes boundaries, and I do mean all four types. You will need to have them ready and in place before you talk with your parents. Prepare your external boundary so that it can help you filter and manage your parents' response, whether it be an under-response, an over-response, or an angry, vengeful reaction. Be prepared to use this boundary to remind you that your parents' reaction is a product of them and them only, and says little to nothing about you. Let it remind you that you didn't choose to grow up emotionally neglected. Let it remind you that you have fought for and earned your emotional health, and that no one, not even your parents, can take it away from you, because you will not allow it. Let it tell you how very much progress you have made, and that you should be proud of yourself. Be prepared to use this boundary for this situation, and use it well.

Your internal boundary will be needed as well. It will help you talk with your parents in a connecting tone rather than a rejecting one, to maintain your cool, even if they don't, and to choose your words with care. Your physical boundary will allow you to get some physical distance if you need it during or after your conversation. Your temporal boundary will help you keep your old pain in its place while you process what's going on in the moment.

Put Yourself First

As someone with CEN, this is probably a major challenge for you. Your natural inclination is to put other people's needs and feelings before your own, but that will absolutely not work for you in this situation.

Of course, you want to have compassion for your parents while you talk with them about CEN. But having compassion for your parents is not the same thing as putting their needs before your own. It's tremendously important that your primary reason for talking with them is to benefit yourself. And that as you are having the conversation, you keep your own needs in the forefront of your mind. Balance your care and empathy for what your parents are feeling with attention to and compassion for what you are feeling and needing. Talk about yourself and your own experiences. Ask for what you need. Protect yourself. Since you are now aware of emotions and have a better understanding of how they work, you can tap into them and use them as a resource during this important conversation.

Your emotions will tell you when you are reaching your parents, or when to talk more or take a break. Paying attention to what your parents are feeling will help you tailor your message in a way that they can hear. But make sure that every decision you make is based primarily on your needs, and secondarily on theirs.

Set Your Expectations

Setting up your expectations in advance involves not only choosing realistic goals for yourself, but also identifying a reasonable definition of success. Your definition of success is very important when we're talking about this, mostly because when you talk with your parents, you can only influence half of the situation: your half. The rest is in the hands of your parents.

I encourage you to set a very small goal for your first attempt. Depending on your parents' level of emotional awareness, simply letting them know that you are thinking deeply about yourself, your childhood, or your family relationships, may be goal enough for your introductory conversation. Keep in mind that you can certainly have more than one conversation with your parents, and the most successful talks like this almost always start small and progress gradually over time, at the rate that your parents, and you, are willing and able to handle.

Here are some examples of potential realistic goals for your first attempt. Please choose only one. Or, since every parent/child relationship is different, come up with your own small goal that is suited to your own personal situation.

Examples of a Realistic Goal for Your First Talk

- They listen to you talk about yourself in a meaningful way for 5 minutes
- They hear the term "Emotional Neglect"
- They share a story from their own childhood that involves CEN
- They hear a story from your childhood that involves CEN

- They learn that you are thinking deeply about yourself, your childhood, and them
- They agree to read an article about CEN
- You feel a moment of emotional connection or empathy either for them or from them

Choose Your Setting

Think about the unique personality of your parent or parents, and consider the best place to talk with them. Make sure it's a time when you will have privacy, enough time, and a comfortable place to talk without pressure.

Think about a time of the day, week, month or year when you have the most relaxed or positive feelings between you and your parents. You might ask them to lunch or dinner, invite them over or stop by their house, ask them to take a walk with you or accompany you on an errand. Your individual "best moment" is unique to you and your parents.

Also consider whether it would help to give your parents a heads-up. Saying, "There's something I would like to talk with you about," can give them a clue that something is going on, and this may help them prepare themselves. But with some parents, it can backfire by making them anxious or avoidant. Tune in to your gut. What does it tell you? How does it tell you to approach this?

Some people find it best not to choose the time and place, and to instead wait for the right moment to arise. Sometimes, these "best moments" can't be planned for or set up, and it works fine to wait for it to occur naturally. However, the risk of waiting for the right moment is that it may not happen on its own, or it may take a very long time. It can be painful to be in the position of watching and waiting endlessly for something to feel right between you and your parents. After all, isn't that a re-creation of the way you spent your childhood?

Choose Your Bridge

By "bridge," I mean what you will use to reach out to your parents. You could also think of this as a connector. Keeping your parents in mind, let's try to identify something that your parents might find interesting or validating, or even just tolerable. Let's now think about some ideas, starting from least bold to most bold. As you read this, think about your own parents, and whether you might get through to them with one of these (or your own twist on it).

Possible Bridges: From Most Careful to Least Careful

- **Lead with the positive.** Begin any approach with giving your parent some validation. Share something you appreciate about them, maybe something they gave you in childhood. This can pave the way to talking about either their childhood or your own. Asking your parent some true and personal version of, "How were you able to give me something important that you never got?" can be a great lead-in to what they couldn't give you because they never got it (emotional validation).
- **Give them a moment of empathy.** With this, you try to bring up a topic that might elicit some vulnerable emotion from your parent, even if it's small. Then you let yourself feel for them, and also let them know that you feel for them.
- **Experience an exchange of empathy.** Double the power of the above moment of empathy by sharing a moment of your own vulnerability. Example: "I can imagine how sad/stressful/ difficult that was/is for you. I felt that same way when…" Your goal is one flicker of mutual understanding between you.
- **Ask them about their childhood.** Eliciting your parent's childhood memories can be a pipeline into his true emotional self. If your parent is only willing to talk about the positive, happy things, get him started with that, and then ask a question that pulls him toward an emotion.

- **Give them a teaser.** Try to squeeze one small bridge into the conversation. You could say something like, "I read something that makes me think differently about our family. I'll tell you about it sometime if you're interested."

- **Tell them about an article you read.** Skip the teaser, and start talking about one of the CEN articles from EmotionalNeglect. com or from my PsychCentral.com blog. Start talking about it, but don't apply it to yourself yet. Choose the particular article you use very carefully. If it contains a bridge that might touch your parents in some way, that sets you up for better success.

- **Show them the book *Running on Empty: Overcome Your Childhood Emotional Neglect.*** Ask them to look at it, and let them know you would like to talk about it with them.

- **Tell them something has been bothering you.** Tell them it's making it hard for you to see them and talk with them. If this makes them curious and willing to talk, proceed with care. If you have parents who truly do care about you and value your relationship but simply lack emotion skills, this more streamlined approach may be the best. Ironically it may also be the only option if you have difficult Type 3 Parents. This bolder approach may be the only thing they will hear, or the only way to reach them. It can also bring your relationship to a head in a way that will finally release you, or at least loosen their grip upon you. See May's story below to see how this can work.

Prepare to Help Your Parents with Guilt

Two factors threaten your success and progress in this endeavor of talking with your parents. They are guilt and defensiveness, and they often go together. Your parent may immediately feel that she is being blamed for your problems, or she may immediately jump to feeling that she has failed. Natural responses to either may be to become defensive or to dissolve in a pool of self-blame.

It's important for you to recognize the potential clout of blame, guilt and defensiveness to derail your best-laid plans. It will be vital for you to anticipate your parents having these feelings, and to jump in to prevent or quickly manage any that may arise. The very best way to prevent and manage your parent's guilt is to provide her with plenty of reassurance, understanding, validation and appreciation. Start with the positive bridge, remind her of what she did right, and show understanding of what she was up against. Express compassion for what she didn't get when she was growing up, and share your positive feelings for her. Use these generously and wisely, and they will help her stay with you and hear you. This can maximize the possibility that you can reach your goal.

Portrait of a Healing Parent/Child Relationship

Olive and Her Type 2 (Struggling) Mother

As Olive and Oscar did their incredible work in couples therapy (described in Part 1), Olive made many new discoveries about herself. She realized what she had been missing all her life and why. She realized that her well-meaning, struggling mother had failed to notice her emotional needs while raising her, and that she herself had continued that pattern. She realized that she had married a man who loved her in the same way her own mother (and absent father) did, and that through it all, it had always seemed to her that everything was fine, even though it was not.

One day, Olive broke the routine that she and her mother automatically followed. Instead of appearing at her mom's house on Saturday morning at 11:00, she called her mother Friday and invited her to lunch on Saturday. Olive remembered a birthday lunch at a nearby restaurant several years ago, at which she and her mother had talked briefly about Olive's grandparents. It had felt at the time like an unusually personal, connected conversation, and Olive hoped to recreate some of that feeling this time.

Slightly thrown off by the unexpected change in routine, Olive's mother was nevertheless willing to go out. At the restaurant, Olive could see her mom's spirits rise, and after they placed their orders with the waiter, they both settled in with a glass of white wine. "This is so nice," Olive's mom said. "Almost like it's a special occasion, but it's not."

Olive had planned her bridge carefully, and she knew just what to say. "I remember last time we were at this restaurant, you told me about the time Granddad left for the war, and how you stepped in to do so many of his chores while he was away." (By bringing up her mother's childhood, Olive is opening a pipeline to the past that she hopes to use to connect with her mom.)

"Oh, yes, that was quite something. We had pigs on the farm, and I had the good fortune of being the one to feed them. I'll tell you, they are cute when they're small, but the grown ones are very, very smelly!" Olive's mom said with a chuckle.

"You know, Mom, I was thinking about your story recently, and I was wondering how Gram handled being left there on the farm, alone with three children. Was she overwhelmed with all that responsibility? She must have been so lonely without her husband."

Looking thoughtful and sad for a moment, Olive's mom smiled again and said, "Yes, but at least she didn't have to feed the pigs. She had me for that!"

"Yes, true," Olive said, laughing with her. "Did you really hate that job so much? Did you ever complain about it?"

"No, I didn't. You know, complaining was not an option back then. There was too much to do on the farm, and not enough manpower to do it. You just managed, and you never said a word about it. We all did."

"Gee, that sounds like a description of your whole life, Mom. You've never had the luxury of complaining, have you? I always think of you as a real trooper."

Olive's mom looks down at her napkin, seemingly a bit uncomfortable. She is not used to compliments, and isn't sure how to respond. Olive sees that, and wants to make her mother comfortable again, so she steers the conversation away from her mom for a moment.

"Did Gram ever complain? Or did she ever seem exhausted, or overwhelmed?"

Looking thoughtful, Mom says, "Well, let's see, no she never complained. But there was one time that she didn't get out of bed for four days. We were teenagers then, and we all scrambled around trying to get everything done. I was the oldest, so I'd go in and ask her several times every day if she was ready to get up, but she would just roll over and put a pillow over her head so I would leave her alone."

"That must have been so weird for you! What did you think was wrong? Were you freaked out?"

"Yes, we thought she was sick at first but then realized she wasn't. Anyway, after a few days she got up and everything went back to normal. Now that I think about it, that happened several times while your granddad was away. We knew we had to make do, so we did."

Feeling surprised by this window into her mother's childhood, Olive is thrown off her game a bit. But she wants to know more. "Did Gram ever explain why she stayed in bed for four days? Did you ever talk about that?"

"Oh, heavens no. We were just glad when she came out, and everything went back to normal, until the next time it happened."

"It's so interesting to hear this, Mom. I wish you would talk more about your childhood." Looking at her mother, Olive sees a wistful sadness in her eyes. She decides this is an opportunity. "I read an article and a book recently, about how common it is for parents to not explain things or talk about stressful family events and problems with their kids, and how it affects the children."

Olive watches her mother carefully for her reaction. She sees some confusion, mixed with curiosity, mixed with sadness.

"Oh. Well, it's just the way it was, and I turned out all right, don't you think?"

"You certainly turned out strong. As I said, you're a real trooper."

Throughout this experience, Olive did many things well. She chose a small, achievable goal for the initial talk: to feel a moment of empathy for her mother. She anticipated that her mom would continually talk about events and things (chores and pigs) and use action words devoid of emotion. She didn't try to push too hard for her own needs to be met. She used her mother's childhood experience to connect with her, and to illuminate the CEN that her mother grew up with. She validated her mother's experience and how strong it had made her, but not so much as to make her mom uncomfortable. And finally, Olive used less-threatening emotion words, like "exhausted," and "overwhelmed" instead of more in-your-face words like "depressed," when talking about Olive's grandmother. And finally, Olive was emotionally attuned to her mother throughout, responding in exactly the way her mother needed to keep the conversation going.

In reading this interaction, you may think that this was an unsatisfying exchange for Olive. After all, she didn't get to talk about her own childhood, and the words Emotional Neglect were never used. In truth, Olive felt a sadness and a longing after this lunch, which she went home and discussed with Oscar.

But this talk was only the first between Olive and her mother. After it, they agreed to have lunch at this restaurant every couple of weeks. And Olive used those lunches to expand on her mother's history. Eventually, she used the term Emotional Neglect to describe her mother's experience, and her mother agreed to read the book. When she did, she recognized how CEN travels through generations, from well-meaning parent to child, and so on.

Olive's mother never really did the work to heal herself from CEN, but Olive could see that she was experiencing more varied emotion, at least during their talks if not at other times as well. Eventually, they ended up talking about Olive's childhood. And for the first time in Olive's life, she and her mother began to feel a true emotional connection that can only happen when two people genuinely see and understand each other.

Your attempt to talk with your Type 2 Struggling Parent may not go as smoothly as this, and that is absolutely fine. Everyone's journey is different, just as every Type 2 Parent and every child is different. But if you follow the general guidelines that Olive used and add in plenty of patience and emotional attunement, you can maximize your chances for a positive outcome.

And now, let's find out what happens when Oscar decides to talk with his Type 1, Well-Meaning-But-Neglected Themselves parents.

Oscar and His Well-Meaning-But-Neglected-Themselves Type 1 Parents

As you recall, Oscar used the Feeling Formula to determine that his net result when he saw his parents equaled zero. Based on these results, he began seeing his parents for an outing instead of in their home, and shortened his visits. He also asked Olive to try not to leave him alone with his father too often. All these interventions helped him prevent that bored, empty feeling that had become so familiar over the years.

These strategies helped Oscar manage his relationship with his parents for a good while. But after some time passed, as he watched his parents age, he began to feel empty and sad again about his relationship with them. He had transformed his own marriage from lonely and distant to vibrant, connected and supportive, and some part of him wondered if he should try to make some connection with his parents now, before it was too late. The conversation about the 50th birthday party had been the last straw. He talked it all over with Olive, who made a good point. She said, "Some day when they're gone, are you more likely to regret having tried to reach them and failed, or having never tried to reach them?"

Oscar realized that he had little to lose, and began to develop a plan. He thought about each of his parents, and how his mother seemed slightly less oppressively vacant than his father. He decided to start by talking with her separately.

Considering his mother's personality, he saw that she always seemed to come alive the most when she was either with her grandchildren or talking about them. He decided that he could use the topic of the grandchildren as a pipeline to reach her. Several weeks later, Oscar's father had knee surgery, and Oscar went to help at his parents' house. While his father was sleeping in the other room, he made some tea and, handing his mother a cup, sat down next to her on the couch. Immediately, not surprisingly, she asked him how her grandchildren, Cindy and Cameron, were doing.

Instead of giving his usual, reassuring but superficial answers, today Oscar took a different tack. "They're fine, of course. But Olive and I are a little bit worried about them both, actually. Cindy's still working at that retail job, and at age 26, she needs to figure out a career for herself. She seems to be struggling."

"Oh," Oscar's mom said, looking slightly concerned. "Well, she's a bright girl. She'll figure it out," she said in the tone she always used to pave over problems. Again, Oscar did the unexpected. He ignored his mother's paving efforts, and continued talking about the problem.

"I've never told you about this, but Cameron started having panic attacks in middle school. He still has problems with anxiety sometimes now." Oscar paused here to observe his mother's reaction. He saw that slight concern come across her face again.

"Well now, what exactly is that?" she asked.

After describing panic attacks to his mom, she nodded thoughtfully. "You know, I used to have those when you kids were little," she explained. "They were terrible. I went to the doctor, and they said it must be stress or something, I don't know." After a pause, thinking deeply, suddenly she said, "Do you think those run in the family? I think my mother had them too! What if Cameron inherited them from me!"

Here, Oscar saw his opening. "The research does show that anxiety runs in families, but I also read an article about some other things that can cause it. When Olive and I were trying to help Cameron, we read a bunch of things and we realized that we made some mistakes raising Cindy and Cameron that probably are contributing to these problems they're having now." Checking his mother's expression, he saw that she looked a bit confused, and didn't know what to say. He decided that he should push forward a little bit.

"Yeah, so this article I mentioned was about how common it is for families to not talk about things, or not pay attention to each other's feelings enough, and believe it or not it can make the kids more likely to have problems with depression or anxiety."

"Well...um...hm...I don't know. I don't get it," Oscar's mother stammered.

"Oh, that's okay Mom, I know it sounds weird. I'll tell you what, I'll email you the article and you can read it and then let me know if it makes sense. Deal?"

Seemingly relieved to be done with the topic, Oscar's mom said, "Well, absolutely. Sure. I'll definitely read it, no problem."

Oscar accomplished a lot in his first attempt with his mother. He talked about a personal, real topic with her, he got some new information about her past and her mother's past, and he introduced the general idea of Emotional Neglect (without naming it). And he also got her to agree to read an article that would explain CEN to her via a topic that was personal to her (anxiety).

After Oscar's mother read the article, she called him right away. She told him about a painful event from her childhood that her parents never talked about or helped her with. Oscar felt genuine empathy for his mother's experience. Over several different talks, he shared with his mother his own experiences with her and his father. Oscar reassured her and helped her with her feelings of self-blame, and she was able to acknowledge that she had failed Oscar emotionally, and to genuinely see how it had affected him. She read some material about Emotional Neglect, and convinced Oscar's dad to read it too.

Oscar's dad never fully connected with the CEN concept, although he did seem to become somewhat more emotionally aware through the process of his wife changing. But Oscar's relationship with his mother changed drastically, as did Olive's relationship with her. Now they both looked forward to visiting Oscar's parents, and felt no need to manage or curtail their time with them. They talked more openly and on a far more meaningful level not only about the grandchildren, but also about the past and their current issues and struggles. And perhaps most importantly, Oscar seldom experienced that old empty boredom that had been his constant companion throughout his life with his parents.

So far, we've seen examples of talking with well-meaning parents about CEN. As you saw, even Well-Meaning and Struggling Type Parents typically require great care, patience and attunement if you are to be successful. But when you have Self-Involved Type 3 Parents, everything is different.

May and Her Self-Involved Parents

The last time we checked in with May, she had turned down her mother's Thanksgiving dinner invitation, and had experienced her mother's revenge of no calls for several months. May had felt selfish for setting limits with her parents, and had managed those feelings quite well through that experience. But as she continued to try to set limits with her parents over time, she realized that it was draining the energy that she needed to preserve for being a healthy mother, a caring wife and an effective attorney. She could see many decades stretching out before her filled with painful and exhausting push/ pulls, limit-setting, and revenge-taking. She realized that she needed to do something to change her relationship with her parents in a real and substantial way.

Since May's mother was so self-focused and vengeful, May was filled with trepidation at the idea of doing anything to challenge her. So she decided to consult with me for some professional advice and support. Together, and with the help of Marcel, we shaped a plan.

May took into consideration the fact that her mother was the primarily self-focused one, and that her father was kinder and less difficult. Sometimes he even seemed to be on her side when she looked into his eyes, but he rarely ever said a word to defend her. May knew that if she talked to her father about CEN, it would accomplish nothing since he would never stand up to her mother. She thought it best to treat them as a unit, and talk to them together.

When I talked with May about this, I warned her that her goal could not be a connecting one (like Olive's and Oscar's). Instead, May's goal was to explain to her parents her reasons for spending less time with them. This was the only way to establish real boundaries and space for herself to live her own life, in her own way, free from the endless cycle of pain and blame inflicted upon her by her parents.

May turned the tables on her parents. Instead of refusing an invitation from them, she called them and invited them to her house for a Sunday afternoon. "There's something I'd like to talk with you about in person," she told them. May's parents were so happy to be asked to their daughter's home, after months of her distancing herself from them, that they said yes immediately.

When May's parents arrived at her house, they were on their best behavior. Chastened by their daughter's recent boundaries, they each gave her uncharacteristically warm hugs in greeting, and May's mother said almost nothing sharp, critical or controlling to her as they had their coffee. This made it more difficult for May to talk with her parents (she began feeling selfish about the prospect of hurting them, and doubting whether this was really necessary), but she knew that she must persevere. After listening to her mother talk endlessly about her important role on the Town Committee, May said, "Mom and Dad, as I said, there's something I want to talk with you about." May's mother stopped talking and looked directly at May, her curiosity taking over her need for attention for the moment.

Marcel sat down next to his wife and took her hand. He knew that May's next words would be difficult for her, and he wanted to make it clear that he was with her on this—clear to May's parents but also, more importantly, to May. He watched May take a deep breath, and waited in admiration for her to begin.

"I know things have been difficult lately, Mom and Dad," May said. "We've been spending a lot less time with you than in years past. And I want to explain to you why that is, because I know your feelings have been hurt, and that hurts me terribly."

May's parents were listening because they felt a moment of empathy from May and could not help being caught up in it. May looked at each of her parents and noticed that her father's eyes were open and vulnerable, whereas her mother's were wide and needy, as they each waited for May to continue. "Mom, you do many good things for me and for Marcel, and especially for the children. But almost every time I'm with you, my feelings get hurt. I finally reached a point where I was getting hurt so often and so much that I needed to take some space, and spend less time with you. I know that's hurt your feelings, and that's why I wanted to explain it to you."

Watching her parents, May saw that her father looked ashamed, and her mother looked defensive and angry. She braced herself for what she knew was coming.

"You are so over-sensitive," May's mother said angrily. "You've been that way since you were a child. I can't believe that taking you on lovely vacations, helping you with the kids, all the great things you say I do for you aren't enough to earn your love. I'm sorry if I can't be the 'ideal' mother, but I try my best, and I think that's all anyone can ask of their mother!" At this point, May's mom was dissolving into tears of righteousness, while her father was looking at the floor.

"I'm sorry this hurts you, Mom. Actually, none of this is about love. Of course I love you, but I simply can't continue to allow myself to get hurt over and over again. It's not good for me. If you ever want to ask me for examples, or find out what you do that's hurtful to me, I'll be happy to talk with you about it. But for now, since you're so upset, maybe we should stop talking about this."

After waiting a few moments to see if May's mom would express curiosity about how she'd been hurting her daughter, Marcel realized that none was forthcoming. So he stood up and said, "Where are those kids of ours? Let me call them in from the back yard so we can all have some cookies." May looked at Marcel with eyes full of gratitude and relief as she too stood up, grabbed a tissue to wipe her own tears, and followed him into the kitchen.

I'm willing to bet that right now you probably are not viewing May's interaction with her parents as a success. But it was a huge accomplishment. In fact, it changed everything for her, but in a very different way than Olive's and Oscar's conversations did.

First, let's review all the things May did right in this talk. First, she chose a challenging but very achievable goal: to express to her parents that their interactions with her were hurtful, and that this was the reason for her recent distancing. Besides choosing a reasonable goal, she also invited her parents to come to her own house, which helped them feel wanted, and set them up to be in the most receptive mode possible.

Turning the tables on your Type 3 Parents who are chasing or trying to smother or control you is a good way to throw the relationship off-balance. When a self-involved or controlling parent is thrown off his game, he can be briefly more open and reachable, and this was May's hope and plan. As you can see, it did allow May to say what she needed to say.

After this intervention, May's relationship with her parents was transformed in a small but crucial way. Her parents remained the same in that their personalities were not, of course, changed. But there were some clear ways in which they interacted differently with their daughter. May's mother was less demanding in her invitations, and less aggressive in shaming her for not spending enough time with them. But the most important difference took place inside of May. She felt strong from having stood up to her parents in an adult manner. She felt freed by her honesty. She felt that she had done her half of what people do in adult relationships, and was no longer responsible for her parents' feelings, reactions and needs. The ball was now in their court.

Although all of this was greatly helpful, it did not solve May's problems with her parents. There were multiple serious continuing issues and struggles, which leads us to our next topic.

What to Do If There Is No Hope

Not all unreachable parents are as difficult as May's. Yours may be fully benign, not at all controlling, accusing, manipulative or aggressive but nevertheless incapable of talking about anything significant. Your unreachable parents may simply be too emotionally fragile or angry to bring up CEN with them. They may be estranged, or already passed away.

No matter the reason, being unable to reach your parents leaves you to cope with all the fallout on your own. You may be left alone, feeling empty. You may feel pressure to forgive your parents, no matter whether they are living or already gone. You may find yourself continually hoping or wishing your parents were different.

The Emptiness You Are Left With

It's natural to think that the only way to fill that emptiness inside of you is to finally receive the warmth and connection from your parents that has been denied you. In truth, although that may be a streamlined "fix," there are other possible ways that will work just as well, and in some cases, even better. If you already understand how Emotional Neglect works, you already know that your emptiness is partially a result of your feelings being pushed away. One key way to fill your empty space is to go through the process of recovering your own emotions, valuing them and listening to them.

Another way to fill your emptiness is to begin to loosen any rigid self-protective walls you still have. These are a product of your childhood, when you needed to protect yourself from your own emotions and your own emotional needs because they were not welcome in your childhood home. Now that you're an adult, you no longer need that wall. You are surrounded by people who are willing to fill your emptiness with their love, warmth and care. Is it your spouse, your sibling, your cousin, a co-worker or friend? It's important to do your best to let those people in. And also, to seek out more of them. To do this, put yourself out there and meet people. Look for those who are trustworthy and who click with you. Then begin to nurture that connection. Be sure to focus on quality of connection, not quantity of connections, for it is the depth of the mutual feeling that will fill you, not the number of people.

The Pressure to Forgive

Everywhere you look there is someone talking or writing about forgiveness. It is frequently touted as the answer for all who have been wronged. "Forgive your parents, or you will become bitter," you will hear from others. Your complicated, painful feelings about your parents may be labeled a "grudge" by those who subscribe to this simplistic view.

Yet it is incredibly difficult to forgive someone who has not recognized how they have wronged you, apologized, or attempted to make things right. I hope that you will not cave to the expectations or one-dimensional advice of others. I hope that you will instead honor your own feelings and work with them and through them in a real way.

If your parents have done *enough* toward trying to correct their relationship with you, then you will likely work your way through to some level of forgiveness, and it will happen naturally. If you are working very hard at forgiving, let this be a sign that you need something more from them. If your parents have not done enough, then forgiving them is not the issue. I suggest that your time and energy and care be redirected away from forgiving, and instead toward coping. And I will offer you plenty of help with that as you read on.

The Forever Wish That Your Parents Could Be Different

If this is you, I want to assure you that all your feelings are perfectly normal and are shared by thousands upon thousands of fine people like you. In fact, I hear this wish so often and from so many people that it begins to seem to me that it is a part of the human condition. YOU ARE NOT ALONE.

I wish that I could tell you something that would help you to free yourself of this wish, but I do believe that this wish is buried so deeply in our humanity that it persists on its own, no matter how well your conscious mind recognizes its futility. So instead of trying to help you erase it, I want to help you manage it. In this regard, I offer you three hints: accept this wish as part of your humanity; know that you share it with many others; don't let this wish make you vulnerable to your parents.

I have witnessed many folks put themselves in emotional harm's way with their parents, driven by this unconscious wish that their parents might change. "*If I just—fill-in-the-blank—maybe my father will finally see me.*" Being aware of your natural wish and realizing that you must manage it with your conscious mind will make you far less vulnerable.

Guilt and the Fear of Being Selfish

Your guilt, that painful feeling that you are doing something wrong, is probably different from the guilt of those who do not have CEN. Why? Because your particular brand of guilt is often driven by the fear of being selfish that is so common amongst CEN folks. Your tendency to focus excessively on other people's needs makes you unnecessarily prone to feeling selfish and guilty. Your guilt feelings interfere with your ability to set limits with your parents and protect yourself. In addition, you have the media as well as millions of people believing that everyone should love their parents. Let me assure you that you are probably the last person who deserves to feel selfish or guilty.

How can you take the necessary steps to set boundaries with your parents, to say "no" to them, or to take up more space with them when your feelings of guilt are telling you that it's wrong? This makes guilt one of the biggest roadblocks for the emotionally neglected.

Taking all those things into consideration, I want to remind you that it is your responsibility to protect yourself from your parents. So make decisions like time spent with them, amount shared with them, and vulnerability to them, with primary attention to your own needs. You are not obligated to give your parents more emotional connection than they have given you. And striving to produce feelings of warmth and love that are not there, simply because others tell you that they should be, will take a huge bite out of your emotional strength and health. In this relationship, I say to you with 100% certainty that you must put yourself first.

Grieve

One of the biggest things that can hold you back in this situation is not allowing yourself to grieve what you will never have. When you finally realize that your parents will never be able to know and love you in the way that they should, there is a good deal of pain involved. To use any of the strategies we are talking about here, you must do some grieving. Allow yourself to feel the sadness and the ache. Allow yourself to cry. You are experiencing a loss that in some ways is greater than a death. Many with emotionally unreachable parents grieve what they will never have so much while their parents are alive that they have no more tears left when they physically lose their parents. And that is all healthy, adaptive, and absolutely okay.

The good thing about grief is that it's not a permanent state, as long as you allow yourself to go through it. That means feel it, process it with your brain, and talk about it with someone who cares. Let a therapist or a trusted partner or friend sit with you in your grief. Taking these steps will finally allow you to move on.

Coping Strategies

It's sad when coping with your parents is a significant challenge in your life. It's even sadder if that challenge begins to take you down, making you feel that you're not good enough, eating away at your self-esteem, or holding you back from taking on other, healthier challenges that could lead you toward strength and growth. That is the last thing I want for you, and the last thing you want for yourself.

In addition to the self-protection strategies we talked about earlier in this section of the book (please do go back and review them again), I want to suggest a few more specifically tailored you, with your unreachable parents.

1. **Focus on Being Yourself.** When you are with your parents, but also as you go through your life, put an extraordinary focus on being yourself. Stop hiding who you are, and let your parents, and others, see the real you. As you read this you may not realize that you've been hiding, but I'm willing to bet that you have. You've been hiding from your parents and others because you

haven't felt accepted *enough* in your childhood home. Which feels more tolerable to you: hiding your light by pretending to be less than you are to avoid ruffling feathers with your family, or letting your true self show, thereby risking an awkward reaction, conflict, or possibly even rejection?

The answer is different for different people. There is no "right" way to do this. In your unique situation, with your unique parents, is it better for you to hide? Or is it better for you to declare yourself? I hope you will go back and re-answer that question periodically, as it may change over time.

If your parents have been abusive to you, or if a fear of being selfish, or feelings of guilt and obligation prevent you from setting much-needed limits with them (or all of the above), letting them see the real you can be a way to turn the tables on them. Just as May did in the example above, letting them know more about your values, your feelings, your needs and your accomplishments can put the ball in their court so that they will find you far less rewarding to engage with. They may become less needy or less demanding, as May's parents did with her. This can be oddly comforting to a CEN person who finds it very hard to say "no." In some cases, it's easier to be rejected than it is to be the rejecter.

2. **Be Cordial.** Whether you decide to become more visible to your parents or prefer to keep a head-down, under-the-radar profile, one simple coping strategy can sustain you. It's straightforward, and almost everyone can do it, yet it has great power to establish and maintain boundaries with CEN parents. It's nothing other than cordiality. If, before you see your parents, you put on your cordial hat, you will be able to relate in a kind, non-confrontational way that also protects you. "Yes, thank you." "Great, and how are you?" "Can I get you a cup of coffee?" "How did your committee meeting go?"

All these cordial statements can feel like love to CEN parents, and yet they cost you little to nothing.

Before we move on to our final strategy, one more word about the significance of abuse. Abusive parents are in a special category. If you have difficulty protecting yourself from parental abusiveness of any kind, please see a therapist for help. This is one of the most challenging situations that a CEN adult can find himself in, and it can destroy you if you allow it. I hope you will seek a licensed, qualified professional to support and strategize with you so that you can prevent your parents from damaging your life.

3. **Pay It Forward.** Now, last but not least, this next strategy is important. It's powerful and it can inspire every area of your life. Take all your frustration and anger, disappointment, guilt, emptiness and grief, and instead of directing it as negative energy backward toward your parents, transform it into positive energy and channel it forward, into your future.

Use it to pay the debt you feel you owe your parents by growing far beyond them. Rebel against those forces that are trying to weigh you down and hold you back. Break through your wall, feel your feelings, own your mistakes. Show empathy to those you care about, and take the risk of loving deeply. Follow your gut, believe in yourself, and make your voice heard. Try your hardest to give your children what you never got yourself. Be you, and know that you are good enough.

This will be the formula to fill your empty space and heal your grief. This will be your way to honor your parents, and pay the ultimate respect to what they *were* able give you.

Your life.

PART 3

YOUR CHILDREN

Chapter 10

THE EMOTIONALLY NEGLECTED CHILD, A PORTRAIT

The CEN Child

May and Marcel—Martha, 6

There's no denying it, *six-year-old Martha is adorable. With shoulder-length ebony hair and dark, almond-shaped, sparkly eyes, she vibrates with life and energy. Martha is May and Marcel's second child, and she keeps them both moving, allowing never a dull moment in their household.*

May and Marcel love Martha's energy and spirit, but they must admit that she can be exhausting. Martha's older brother, 11-year-old Michael, is more similar in nature to his parents. He is far quieter and calmer than Martha. Marcel sees his daughter's energy as engaging and connecting. May, however, often feels overwhelmed by it. Marcus describes Martha's energy as her "spark," whereas May describes it as "intensity."

Both Marcel and May are somewhat confused about the strength of their child's emotions. When Martha is happy, she is a delightful, creative bundle of joy. But when she gets upset, she can go from 0 to 60 in what feels like one second. A frown becomes a crumpled face becomes loud screaming and crying in an instant.

Marcel spends long days at his job, and travels for work a few weeks out of every month, so his exposure to his daughter's spark is minimal. This leaves May, who grew up with an emotionally abusive and neglectful mother, to grapple with their daughter's powerful feelings on her own for much of the time.

May has no idea how to handle her daughter's intense emotions. When Martha was three, May tried giving her time-outs. But that only served to escalate Martha's yelling, and seemed to make her "fits" worse. As Martha got a little older, May tried reasoning with her, but that seemed to have no effect at all. May tried ignoring Martha's fits: same result.

Interestingly, Martha's fits were always more plentiful and intense when Marcel was away. And even more interestingly, she did not have them at all at school. Reports from Martha's teachers were that she was an extremely well-behaved, bright and well-liked student at school.

May and Marcel were at their wit's end. They were worried that Martha should have outgrown her emotional fits by now.

Until finally, one day, Marcel read Running on Empty: Overcome Your Childhood Emotional Neglect.

You might recall that initially Marcel picked up the book because he wanted to understand what he felt was so deeply missing in his marriage. He had always felt confident that he and May were excellent parents. He saw how loving and devoted his wife was with the children, and how careful she was to give parenting everything she had despite her demanding law practice. And although May seldom talked about it, he also saw how careful she was to never pass her own mother's controlling, emotionally abusive parenting on to her own children. As he read the book, however, and began to see his wife and marriage through the lens of CEN, he had also begun to see his children through it as well.

Now, he began to wonder if there was some connection between May's own childhood, what was missing in their relationship, and the problems they were having with Martha.

The realization of CEN often begins like this. First you see it in its most obvious place in your life. Then, as you more fully understand its breadth and depth, you see it in layers all around you. For Marcel, seeing it in his children was the hardest, because he saw all the wonderful things he and May did for the children. He knew how very much they loved them. But he could not see what was not there: *enough* emotional responsiveness and awareness to help an emotionally sensitive child such as Martha learn the limits and emotion skills that she would need in order to thrive.

Fortunately, as you will see, Marcel's realization came with plenty of hope for his own children. This is the silver lining of Childhood Emotional Neglect. It can truly, definitely, without a doubt, be healed.

The CEN Teen

Olive and Oscar—Cameron, 17

Approximately one year before Oscar's talk with his mother about CEN, he and Olive sat in their living room together, talking earnestly. They were trying to make sense of the call they had received from seventeen-year-old Cameron's school that day, and figure out what to do about it.

That morning, Cameron's eleventh-grade history teacher had called to let Olive know that her son seemed to be struggling at school lately. "Cam doesn't seem to be as involved with his friends as he used to be," his teacher said. "I've seen him sitting alone at lunch recently, and he used to be constantly surrounded by several groups of friends. I had been noticing a difference in him lately, but today he wasn't in class, so I went to look for him."

It turns out that Cam's history teacher had found him in the boys' bathroom, hyper-ventilating. It had taken the teacher ten minutes to help Cam calm his breathing and take him to the school nurse's office. "He did come back to class afterward, but he seemed very embarrassed, and he would not talk to me or to the nurse about what happened, or what was going on with him. We thought you should know about it," the teacher said.

After Olive shared this conversation with Oscar, they both slumped sadly in their chairs. They were in the process of working on their marriage at that time, and we were in the midst of the couples therapy that would so deeply change their marriage and their views of themselves. Cam had had several incidents in the past of withdrawal from his friends and of getting "stressed out." But this was the first time that Cam's parents had a deeper understanding of emotions and how they work. This is the first time it was possible for them to truly grasp what was going on with their son.

Before, when Cam had his episodes of struggling, Olive and Oscar thought he was tired and stressed, and overwhelmed by the demands of his schoolwork. They assumed he was taking on too much, and began to enforce earlier bedtimes for him. There were some difficult periods, but he always seemed to snap out of it on his own after a few days. Those prior episodes had not been this dramatic, however. This was the first call from a teacher about hyperventilation, and for the first time, alarm bells were ringing for Oscar and Olive.

In our couples session that week, we talked about Cameron. I knew both Oscar and Olive very well by this point, and I knew that they were loving and caring parents. I also could see very quickly, with my view through the lens of CEN, that Cam was having anxiety attacks, and why. But before we could talk about the "why" or what to do about it, I had to help Oscar and Olive through the pain of their own self-blame.

Since Oscar had been forced to confront the importance of emotion in his life (during his cancer scare) earlier than Olive, *he had been watching his son through a different lens for quite some time. Oscar had looked back on his children's reactions to his cancer surgery and treatment, and had seen that they had not talked about it with Cindy and Cameron in the way that was needed. They had shared the facts and events about the illness, and had kept the children informed of Oscar's health status throughout, but they had not addressed the feelings involved in any substantial way. By the time I saw Olive and Oscar to talk about Cam's anxiety attack, they had already discussed this thoroughly at home. They were both feeling the weight of responsibility and self-recrimination for having failed their children in this way.*

"It's our fault he's suffering like this," Olive said. And then, out in a tumble of tears came all the observations and realizations they had each been having since they learned about CEN. They talked about how Cindy had been ultra-independent, even as a toddler. As a pre-teen and teenager she seldom seemed to need much help or support from her parents, and they had taken a somewhat hands-off approach raising her. The same theme had, unsurprisingly, carried through Oscar's cancer incident. Cindy had been concerned, of course. But she had seemed very strong and able to handle it. So much so, in fact, that Olive and Oscar had been quite impressed by it.

Cam, on the other hand, had seemed to have a harder time with it. He tended to become teary-eyed when Olive updated him on Oscar's status. Olive had thought it best to reassure him at those times, and had been careful to tell him that everything would be okay; that his dad would be fine (the same strategy she used with Oscar, you may recall). This had seemed to work, as Cam always seemed to recover nicely, nodding in affirmation that he knew everything would be okay. Olive, who was exhausted and terrified throughout the experience, had been relieved that both of her children were so strong and handled the situation so well.

Now, looking back through the lens of CEN, Olive could see that she had been a loving and caring mom to her kids, but that she and Oscar had raised them without enough attention to the emotions underlying their personalities, their reactions, and their everyday lives.

The CEN Child, All Grown Up

Oscar and Olive—Cindy, 26

For years, Oscar and Olive had noticed that Cindy avoided their calls, and skipped opportunities to spend time with them. When they did see Cindy, she could be unpredictably irritated with them over seemingly small things. In high school, they'd assumed her avoidance and irritability was typical teen behavior. But in college, she continued to snap at them. Also, they noticed that when other students went home to their family for breaks, Cindy frequently chose to stay on campus instead. They had always viewed this as "independence" on Cindy's part, and they saw her lack of a need to come home as a sign of strength. They had sometimes talked about how proud they were of Cindy's independence, and had been unaware that they also felt a bit sad and rejected at the same time.

Cindy had a bachelor's degree in business, a major that she had chosen out of desperation her junior year. Her college required her to declare, and Cindy had no idea what she wanted to study. Cindy's parents had been quite surprised to hear that she had chosen business, but she became annoyed when they'd asked her about it. So, at the time, Olive and Oscar had dropped it.

Now, at 26, Cindy had been finished with college for several years. She was living in Providence, Rhode Island, about an hour and a half from her parents' home in Boston. She was living with several roommates, and had obtained a sales job at a jewelry store, where she had worked for three years, post-college. She had been promoted to evening manager of the store, and seemed to enjoy working there. But her parents worried that she was not on a true career path, and that she wasn't taking full advantage of her college degree.

As Olive and Oscar began to see their children through the lens of CEN, they had for some time been thinking more deeply than ever before about their relationship with Cindy. They had begun to question if her snaps were a sign of deeper anger at them, and if her extreme independence signified something other than strength. Realizing that Cindy felt little need to see or interact with them, they also saw that when they were together, her communication with them seemed devoid of meaningful conversation.

"How's your job going, Cindy?" Oscar would ask. "Great," Cindy would respond. It was predictable and rote, and as a result, Oscar and Olive had very little insight into the true nature of Cindy's life. They began to see that Cindy's relationship with them carried some similar hallmarks of their relationships with their own parents. They began to see glimmers of a connection that had failed to form between themselves and their daughter. Finally, they understood what may be wrong, and why. Now all they needed to do was manage their own emotional reactions in this situation, and figure out what to do about it.

The lens of CEN can be, at times, uncomfortably powerful. Once you begin to view yourself, your childhood, your relationships, and finally, your children through this lens, you may begin to feel the earth shifting under your feet. But none of these realizations is as heavy as the "parent lens." Once you're looking through it, you are faced with many painful realities that can set you back. This was indeed happening for Oscar and Olive, and had been for quite some time. The incident at Cam's school wasn't the beginning for them, it was only the catalyst that forced them to talk about it openly with each other and me. And it forced them to feel it in a way they had never felt it before.

As you and I can readily see, Oscar and Olive love their children and want the best for them. They have used all the tools in their toolboxes to raise them maximally well. The pain and guilt they are feeling at this point is very understandable, but for those reasons, it is misplaced. And it threatens to derail them if they allow it to do so. We'll talk about how that went for Oscar and Olive later, but first we must discuss your feelings as a parent.

Chapter 11

THE FEELINGS OF THE CEN PARENT

> " *Like the gift that keeps on giving, CEN automatically transfers from one generation to the next.* "

Before we start talking about fixing anything in your parenting, I want you to understand yourself, and your own parenting, better. You may wonder why this matters. You may feel compelled to jump straight to the fix. You may feel that your feelings are a side factor, and pale in importance compared to your children's. In fact, since you have CEN, you may be tempted to skip this chapter altogether.

To this, I say: Don't even think about it.

I cannot allow you to treat yourself as if your feelings don't matter. In addition, as you may at this point realize, changing your actions is far easier when you are aware of your feelings.

What happens when your parents have emotional blind spots? They are blind to at least some of your emotional needs as they raise you. The natural result is that you grow up to be blind to your own emotions. And so it continues. Like the gift that keeps on giving, CEN automatically transfers from one generation to the next.

Yes, it is truly automatic. When your parents failed to notice or respond to your feelings, or failed to see and respond to your true nature, they unwittingly set you up to be unaware of your feelings as you parented your own children. But trust me, you have been having many, many feelings as you've raised your own children. Perhaps you've been aware of some of your feelings, and perhaps you've even felt guilty about having them.

Have you wondered if your feelings as a parent are in the normal range? Have you read articles about parenting, and felt they didn't quite capture your own parenting issues or struggles? If so, it may be because those articles did not take into account the effects of *what you didn't get* as a child. And those effects, not surprisingly, are tremendous.

As you probably know, there are ten particular characteristics that result from CEN. These are the ten struggles that challenge the CEN adult. Perhaps you've already thought about the role of the ten CEN characteristics in your life, and if so, that will be helpful. If you haven't, that's okay. You will still be able to consider them as you apply them to your parenting experience.

Now let's look more deeply into the ten classic CEN challenges, and apply them, very specifically, to your feelings as a parent. In this comprehensive description of the feelings of CEN parents, some will strike a chord with you, and others will not. Please pay attention to the feelings you have as you read them, as your feelings in the moment will inform you of the ones that are true and meaningful to you. Keep in mind that it may feel uncomfortable to read about some of these feelings. Let me give you three reminders to help you manage that discomfort while you read the next section.

Three Reminders (Well, Four)

1. **You can't choose your feelings.** They are part of your biology, and a product of your past and current situation.

2. **Feelings are not subject to moral judgments.** The concept of right and wrong does not apply to emotions. Never judge yourself for having a feeling.

3. **Becoming aware of, and accepting, a feeling is vital.** Awareness of what you are feeling is essential, of course. But you must also

accept that you have the feeling, even if you don't like it. These are the first steps to being able to manage it.

One More Reminder: All parents have uncomfortable feelings about their role as a parent, and about their children. Few express these feelings outwardly because they are afraid others will judge them. Never let yourself feel ashamed for having any of the feelings you read about below. You are in the good company of legions of loving, caring parents who are very much like yourself.

The Feelings of the CEN Parent

1. **Counter-Dependence**: A grave fear of depending on other people.

You were set up for this fear in your childhood. When you needed help as a child, and no one noticed, you received a subliminal lesson. You learned that relying on others is bad, or shameful. And you learned that if you expect help from others, you will end up disappointed.

Have you ever looked around at other parents, and felt mystified about how comfortable they seemed with their children's neediness? Some parents seem to even thrive on it. But depending on how your parents responded to your needs as a child, that may seem practically unfathomable to you.

As a parent, your counter-dependence can set you up to feel, on some level, deeply uncomfortable with the dependence that is naturally built into your relationship with your child. Your own needs were thwarted as a child, and now a small being has lots of needs that you are required to fulfill. You may feel, on some deep or even unconscious level, that this is an unfair bind to be placed in. And now that we're talking about this openly, I want to assure you that your feeling makes a lot of sense and is valid. You are indeed in an unfair bind. On top of that, society tells you (by seldom airing any negative feelings about parenting) that your feeling of being in an unfair bind is not how a parent is supposed to feel.

In addition to the bind, your fear of relying on others may make it difficult for you to ask for help and accept help. All parents get overwhelmed and exhausted at times, and need support and assistance. If relying on other caretakers makes you feel vulnerable or weak or selfish, you will find yourself running on empty.

The Feelings You Are Left With: Caught in a bind, unfairness, deep discomfort with your child's dependency on you, and possibly some guilt or shame about that. Depleted, and running on empty.

2. <u>**Poor Self-Compassion**</u>: An impaired ability to empathize with yourself, recover from mistakes, understand and sympathize with your own struggles, and cut yourself some slack.

If your parents didn't show you enough compassion as a child, you didn't learn how to feel it for yourself. You become your own harshest critic. Then, when you take on this most difficult job in the world, you are set up to experience some very harsh judgments—your own.

Is there a little voice in the back of your head, telling you that you're not a good enough parent? Telling you you're not as giving as other parents? Judging you for not caring enough, not feeling enough, or not doing enough? Do you expect near-perfection from yourself as a parent, regardless of the factors that stand in your way? Do you feel selfish when you put your own needs before your children's? Lacking self-compassion is a sure way to find yourself feeling inadequate.

The Feelings You Are Left With: Inadequacy, selfish, judged, deserving of judgment, criticized, guilty.

3. <u>**Emptiness**</u>: A deep sense that something is missing in you. You may experience it as numbness, a lack of feeling, or actual emptiness.

As a child, you had to wall off your feelings so they would not interfere in your childhood home. Now, as an adult, you are living without enough access to your emotions. This leaves you with a deep sense that something is missing inside you.

As a parent, you are of course supposed to love your children. You're supposed to feel a deep caring for them. And you know these feelings are there, within you. But you don't always feel them in the way that other parents seem to feel them. Generally, your children may fill some of the empty space left by your own childhood, with their emotions, their brightness, and their vivid intensity. But in other ways, they may also make you even more aware of what you are missing.

You may experience moments when you go to the well, looking for some feeling for your children, and find that there's not enough there. At that moment, you may catch a glimpse of an absence of something, and it may feel deeply uncomfortable.

The Feelings You Are Left With: Wanting to give, but the well feels dry. Troubled. Ashamed. Sad. Deficient. Exhausted.

4. **Inaccurate Self-Appraisal**: A lack of specific, realistic, balanced self-knowledge.

Every child develops a clear sense of who she is when her parents pay attention, and notice who she is. When you are a child, and you look into your parents' eyes and see yourself reflected there, you learn about yourself. When your parent sees that you are a kind-natured and sensitive child, you learn this about yourself. When your parent sees that you tend to feel easily embarrassed, you learn this about yourself. When your parent "gets" that you are serious, bright, shy, sweet, distractible, energetic, reliable, loyal, generous, good at soccer, not so good at track (you get the idea), you "get" this about yourself.

When you grow up looking into your parents' eyes and seeing an inadequate, unclear or inaccurate reflection of yourself, you do not have the opportunity to learn who you are. This sets you up to struggle through life with a lack of information about your true nature. This affects you in many areas of your life, from choosing a career to deciding where to live, to choosing a mate.

As a parent, you will struggle to understand and know your child in the same way that you struggle to understand and know yourself. You may have difficulty understanding your child's true nature, his strengths and weaknesses, preferences, proclivities, temperament and needs.

The Feelings You Are Left With: Lost, confused, puzzled about your child, distant.

5. **Guilt and Shame**: Your "go to" feelings are guilt and shame.

As a child, you essentially parented yourself (in the emotion department at least). Lacking parental input and emotional education, you developed your own "inner parent" voice. Your inner parent voice is likely somewhat simplistic, since it was created by you as a child. In the mind of your inner parent voice, you either do things rightly or wrongly. You are either a good parent or a bad parent. Negative feelings are bad, and perhaps even positive feelings are too. You lack the balanced, clear voice of the adult who can see the complexity of a situation or emotion through the lens of empathy. This set-up is not your friend when it comes to parenting.

As a parent, when you sense a small parental failure on your part (which every parent does), you find yourself unable to sort it through to understand it. Perhaps instead, you go straight to shame. Essentially, you may end up feeling guilty for, or ashamed of, every mistake you make and every imperfection within your own parenting. This type of misplaced shame interferes with your ability to learn from your mistakes, and learning from your own mistakes is a pillar of effective parenting.

The Feelings You Are Left With: Shame, shame and more shame. Guilt, guilt and more guilt. And frustration about it all.

6. **Self-Directed Anger and Self-Blame**: This is an endless cycle that appears everywhere in your life. You are quick to blame yourself, and anger is quick to follow. You blame yourself for all that goes wrong, and you're angry at yourself for that.

Most CEN families do not handle anger well. Anger is not just any old feeling, it's an especially challenging one. Your CEN family probably made one of two possible mistakes with anger. They may have pretended it didn't exist at all, forcing everyone in the family to repress their natural feelings of anger. Or they may have done the opposite, failing to manage their anger so that it ran rampant throughout your childhood home. Either way, you didn't learn how to accept, manage or express your natural anger in a healthy way. This is a big problem, of course, because it's impossible to be a parent without getting angry.

In my experience, most people with CEN, not knowing what to do with their anger, end up turning it toward themselves. As a parent, it's very, very helpful to have a healthy relationship with your anger. Healthy anger motivates you, and informs you about when to set limits with your children, and when you need to take better care of yourself. But instead of helping you, your anger is in your way. Turned toward you, instead of in the direction of its proper targets, it holds you down, drains your energy, and renders you less effective. Because you are holding your anger in, misdirecting and internalizing it, sometimes it may emerge all at once, directed at your children in a way that you know, deep down, is unfair to them. And you find all this confusing and mystifying, of course.

The Feelings You Are Left With: Self-blame, a remarkable absence of anger which may alternate with excessive anger, and guilt. Confusion.

7. **The Fatal Flaw**: A deep sense that something is wrong with you. You are different from other people.

The Fatal Flaw is one of the primary markers of Childhood Emotional Neglect. This powerful "flaw" is in fact only a *feeling of being flawed*. It holds you separate, removed from other people. You become afraid of letting anyone too close to you, in fear that they will see that something is wrong with you, and reject you. The Fatal Flaw can keep you feeling that you don't quite belong anywhere, with anyone.

As a parent, your Fatal Flaw sits under the surface, driving your choices but also affecting your emotions as you parent. It can make you hold yourself separate not only from your partner, but even from your children. Your fear of letting anyone get too close and see the real you can leave your relationship with your children feeling a bit more distant than you suspect it should. The distance feels normal to you in many ways (since it's how you've always lived), but at times you may also feel disappointed in the lack of closeness of your bond with your children.

I have also heard countless CEN parents express discomfort with the many social requirements of being a parent, like school open houses, parent-teacher nights or PTO meetings. That feeling of being on the outside, that interior need to keep yourself separate and protected, leaves you feeling that you somehow don't belong. It can make you feel uncomfortable being visible at a school event, and hard to chit-chat with other parents at baseball games and potlucks. With the Fatal Flaw hidden within you, you may be able to put on your happy face and get by, but it requires a lot of energy, and it often leaves you feeling drained.

The Feelings You Are Left With: Disappointed in your connection with your children, perhaps worried about the connection, anxious, stressed, alone. Out of place, and drained.

8. **Poor Self-Discipline**: The inability to discipline yourself.

Contrary to popular belief, we are not born with the ability to discipline ourselves. We learn it from our parents, when they discipline us as children. Your CEN parents may have failed to offer you enough limits and clear boundaries, delivered in a healthy, balanced way. Now, all grown up, you haven't been able to internalize these healthy skills and use them in a balanced way. Disciplining your own children in a natural way like other parents do is a struggle for you. Just like the emotional blind spots, these blind spots also are passed on from one generation to the next.

Having failed to receive enough limits and boundaries as a child, you may find yourself struggling, feeling helpless and confused about your children's discipline needs. You may end up under- or over-disciplining your children. Neither works very well, but it's hard to see what you are doing wrong.

The Feelings You Are Left With: Out of control, lost, helpless, frustrated, angry at your children for their lack of cooperation, confused.

9. **Difficulty Nurturing Self and Others**: The process of giving and receiving pure, profound, unguarded feelings of love, warmth and care is obstructed.

In order to share and experience these pure feelings as an adult, you must receive them, and be permitted to freely give them, as a child. Truth be told, writing about this particular struggle makes me feel sad. It's because I have a picture in my mind of you as a child, a small boy or girl, naturally, healthfully wanting and seeking what every child needs in a pure and innocent way, but barred from experiencing that open exchange *enough*.

Your natural needs for nurturance were frustrated as a child, and the lesson you learned from that was profound.

Don't freely need, and don't freely take.

As a parent, you love and care for your children, of course! But there exists, somewhere deep in your interior self, a barrier. You may or may not be aware of this barrier, but nevertheless, it is there. There's a good chance that your inner block is a mirror image of one or both of your parents. But if you've become aware of it and worked on your CEN, it has, for sure, been weakened and lowered.

This interior obstruction, hand in hand with your Fatal Flaw, sadly keeps you from being emotionally involved in the most full and complex way possible with your children. It may be difficult for you to sense the effects of your inner block, or to gauge the magnitude of its interference. Yet you live with it each and every day. Your children may experience that same thwarted feeling you grew up with. (Don't feel bad right now, it's not your fault! And you can, and will, fix it.) You may feel a bit thwarted, or obstructed, as well, in your relationship with them.

Your inner obstruction also makes it difficult for you to nurture yourself. As a parent, you may view your own needs as a person, for rest, unstructured time, or self-care, as excessive or selfish.

The Feelings You Are Left With: Blocked, thwarted, distant from your children, selfish, depleted and running on empty.

10. <u>**Alexithymia**</u>: A lack of emotional awareness, knowledge and skills.

Childhood is a training ground for emotional intelligence. When your parents see what you feel and respond to your feelings by helping you name and manage them, you learn what different emotions feel like, and how to put them into words. You learn how to identify what you're feeling, and why you may be feeling it. You learn how to understand why you do what you do, and deduce the reasons for others' actions as well.

Of course, since you didn't receive this kind of attention and training in your own childhood, you weren't able to internalize these valuable skills. Now, when you try to understand your own children, you are operating with a deficit of knowledge. You find yourself wondering why your child is behaving a certain way, and over-focusing on her behavior instead of her feelings. Since it's difficult for you to understand your child on a deeply emotional level, you often feel at a loss in terms of helping her, directing her or giving her what she needs.

The Feelings You Are Left With: Confused, mystified, worried, frustrated.

Summary

I fully realize that it may have been hard for you to read about the many difficult and painful feelings that you have had as a parent. Of course, it's important to acknowledge that all these negative feelings co-exist with many joyful, loving and connected feelings in your role as a parent, as well. Having worked with hundreds of CEN parents, I assure you that, no matter how much self-doubt, shame, or disconnection you feel with your child, there is nothing actually wrong with the intensity, quality or value of your love. It's all there, inside you. You are not lacking anything, and you are not selfish. You do love your children enough. And you do care enough. The problem is only with accessing and sharing what you feel.

Having made it through the entire section above about your feelings, I encourage you at this point to acknowledge and accept that this is your experience. It's what you were handed, most likely unwittingly, by your parents. You didn't ask for any of those feelings, nor did you choose them.

Your experience is valid, and your feelings are real. They are a product of your Childhood Emotional Neglect.

And what do we know about Childhood Emotional Neglect?

It can be healed.

Chapter 12

HOW CEN HAS AFFECTED YOUR PARENTING

> **"** *CEN continues to work its "magic" long after your children are grown.* **"**

We've established that CEN has a profound effect on how you feel within yourself, about yourself, and in relationship with your children as a parent. This is true not only when you are actively parenting your children. Unfortunately, CEN continues to work its "magic" long after your children are grown.

I fully understand that reading the previous chapter, as well as this one, is challenging. I wish I could find a less taxing way to transfer all this vital information to you, because the last thing I want to do is burden you, or make you feel guilty or ashamed. You have had enough of that in your life already. But we know that if we are to change your relationship with your children, we must first understand it. And to understand it, we must talk about it. And I fully understand that you may find talking about some of these things to be hard. I can only hope that you will trust me to walk you through this discovery and recovery path in a way that will be caring, worthwhile, healing and ultimately greatly rewarding.

In the interest of doing that: If you have just finished reading Chapter 11, and you're forging ahead to this chapter, I encourage you to give yourself a little break first. Do something nourishing for yourself, and let your brain process what you have just read. Take a bubble bath or a hot shower, or take a walk and get some fresh air. Have a chat with someone you like, or eat some fresh strawberries. Listen to some music that you love. Or better yet, wait and read this chapter tomorrow. You are in no rush, and it will help you digest this material if you have a little time to process Chapter 11 first.

In this chapter, we will look at your relationship with your children. Of course, we know that every parent/child relationship is unique and complicated. As we talk about your own personal ones, we will not try to capture every aspect of them. Instead, we will focus on the specific footprint that Childhood Emotional Neglect has left on you, how it inserts itself into your specific parenting with your specific child, and how it is likely experienced by your child. Don't expect everything you read to necessarily be true about you, as it all depends on your own unique footprint. And don't worry, throughout this chapter we will take intermittent pauses so that I can remind you of three vital truths:

- **<u>None</u> of the products of CEN are your fault**
- **You are a caring parent (I know that because you are reading this)**
- **It is never too late to heal your relationship with your child**

Let's now look at exactly how each of the ten elements of CEN described in Chapter 11 play out in May and Marcel's relationship with their young children Martha (6) and Michael (11), and in Oscar and Olive's relationships with their children, Cindy (adult) and Cameron (teen). As you read about the experiences of these lovely, caring people and their children, I hope you will be thinking about yourself, your children, and what your children may be feeling.

The Feelings of the CEN Child

The emotions of children are, in many ways, just as complex as those of adults. And in some ways, because they are experienced in perhaps a purer form, they can be even more powerful. Of course, we know that children are subjected to many outside forces every day, and their feelings are not all a direct result of their parents' treatment of them. A child's world is full of people, including teachers and peers. School rules, academic and social pressures, and genetics also play a role in the emotions of a child.

But for our purposes here, we will focus on the direct effect of the parents' CEN struggles upon the child's feelings. Let's now move on to see how Martha, Michael, Cindy and Cameron react emotionally to their parents' CEN characteristics.

1. Counter-Dependence

Martha, 6

> *It's Thursday, a half-day at Martha's elementary school. After the last bell, the children who are not taking the bus home are routinely released onto the playground to run around and play until their parents arrive. On this beautiful day, Martha is deeply involved in a game with her friends on the jungle gym. As Martha sees her friend climbing toward her, she moves away as quickly as she can to escape getting tagged. Laughing and squealing, she barely evades the tag, and at just that moment she hears her mother's voice calling her name, and sees her mother and her brother Michael standing near the school waving at her to come over.*
>
> > *Only halfway through her game, Martha experiences the sight of her mother almost as if someone suddenly threw a wet blanket over her head. Determined to finish her game, she pretends to see and hear nothing, and continues playing. This only works for a minute or so, as May walks over to the jungle gym and says, "Hello, young lady. Let's get your backpack and get going now."*

Realizing she must now obey her mother, Martha is hit with the reality that her fun time is at an end, and that she and her friends will never know the true winner of this game. Suddenly, she feels a deep sense of disappointment and unfairness. Her expression of joy falls immediately into an unhappy frown. "Pleeeeeease, Mom, I have to finish and we're only halfway," she begs. But looking at her mother's face, she sees that this is a losing battle, and a hopeless cause. Falling dramatically from the jungle gym, she screams, cries, and yells her disappointment to all who are nearby.

Feeling embarrassed, May stands next to Martha, watching helplessly. Exhausted from a particularly stressful morning at work, she is thinking about how Martha seems to know the days that she is most depleted, and chooses them to throw her fits.

In the midst of her yelling and crying, Martha sneaks a peek at her mother to gauge her reaction. She sees a stony, frozen expression, and realizes that her mother is not even looking at her. "She doesn't even care!" Martha thinks miserably. Feeling further enraged, more wails ensue.

In this scenario, May has done nothing wrong. In fact, she has gone to extraordinary measures to do everything exceedingly right. Since every Thursday was a half-day at her children's school, every Thursday she left her busy law practice in the middle of the day to pick up her kids and work from home for the afternoon. May and Marcel had discussed having their neighbors pick up Michael and Martha when they pick up their own kids on Thursday, or having the kids go to the after-school program for a few hours. But May was too uncomfortable to ask the neighbors for this favor, as she didn't want to feel indebted to them. And she didn't feel it was right to have the children go to the after-school program, when they could be at home with her, doing their homework and playing in the yard.

May held her ground on this against Marcel's best attempts to convince her. She continued to pick up the kids on Thursdays, even though the managing partners at her firm took a dim view of it, and would pile more work on her every Friday morning, seemingly to discourage her from continuing it.

May doesn't realize that she is caught in the counter-dependence trap. May's narcissistic mother typically put her own needs before May's, so May is highly accustomed to having her needs thwarted. This makes it feel natural to her to be squeezed from both ends, between her job and her children. May is afraid to rely on others for help, so she avoids it at all cost. She automatically takes on too much, trying to be everything to everyone, while sacrificing her own needs in the process.

Martha is, of course, completely unaware of any of her mother's issues and struggles. She only has one healthy, honest child's need that's pure and simple and clear. And that is to have her mother notice and respond to her feelings and needs. Not by indulging them, but by seeing them, acknowledging them, and helping her to manage them.

2. Low Self-Compassion

Cameron, 17

Cameron sat in his high school chemistry class, taking a test. Having answered four of the questions fairly confidently, there were two remaining that he was having difficulty making sense of. "I didn't study this part of the electrochemical principles," he thought to himself. "How did I miss that?" This realization then blossomed into an attack on himself.

"How do I always manage to study the wrong thing! I don't know what my problem is." Looking around, Cameron noted that the students around him seemed to be hard at work, and looked like they understood what they were doing. "Everyone else must have studied the principles. I'll be the only one that made this stupid mistake," he continued, entering into alarm mode.

During this entire thought process, Cameron was not aware that his heart rate was increasing, and his thoughts were also increasing in speed. With his heart racing and his catastrophic thinking escalating, time passed at lightning speed. Suddenly, Cam looked at the clock and realized that his teacher was about to call, "Time's up. Hand in your papers."

Cameron handed in his paper and, with his head down in hopes that no one would try to talk to him, he walked as far away from his group of friends as possible, heading rapidly home. By the time he reached the door of his house, tears were brimming in his eyes.

When he walked in the door, he noticed his mother rushing around the house, gathering things up. "Hey Cam, how was school today?" she called from another room. Before he could answer, she walked toward him carrying several items and said, "I'm on my way to Grandma's house. I'll be home before dinner." After his mom rushed out of the house, Cam collapsed on his bed and put his headphones on. He blasted music as loudly as he could stand it, in hopes of drowning out the harsh anger he was feeling at himself, and the critical voice in his head saying, "You screwed up again."

All students make mistakes in their studying, and all parents rush around sometimes, so in many ways, this story is unremarkable. But it highlights the damage done by the harsh self-judgment, accusations and anger that result from a lack of self-compassion. How did Cameron develop such a harshness with himself? He, unfortunately, was inadvertently taught it by his parents.

Remember Cameron's mother, Olive's, relationship with her mother? Olive grew up taking care of her siblings so that her own mother could work. Now, as an adult, she acts as caretaker to her elderly mother. Olive grew up with little awareness of her experiences and feelings from her over-taxed, exhausted mom and absent father. No one noticed Olive's mistakes when she was growing up, and talked her through them. There was no reasonable, balanced adult voice in her life, helping her sort through what went wrong, and how it went wrong, or what she could do differently the next time. I call this voice "Compassionate Accountability."

Compassionate Accountability: A caring, reasonable internal voice that coaches you through mistakes and helps you make choices. It holds you accountable, but in a compassionate way. It neither lets you off the hook, nor judges you. It helps you learn from your mistakes and choices, put them behind you, and move on. To learn more about how to cultivate this voice in yourself, see my previous book, *Running on Empty, Overcome Your Childhood Emotional Neglect.*

Since neither Olive nor Cameron's dad, Oscar, grew up with a voice of Compassionate Accountability, neither parent has it to give to Cameron.

So Cameron has grown up with no one coaching him enough through his choices or mistakes. Cameron knows only one "coping" technique, and that is to attack himself. It is, of course, not only ineffective, but also self-damaging. In fact, he was so busy doing it that he lost valuable time on the test, which he could have used to perhaps figure out the missed questions. Imagine if Cameron's interior voice had instead said, "Uh oh, you missed the electrochemical principles. That's not good. But it's okay, everyone makes mistakes. Focus, focus, and you can figure this out." He could have then applied all his self-attack, anxiety-producing energy toward solving the problem at hand.

One other aspect of this story is important to mention. When Cameron walked through the door with tears in his eyes, his rushing mother didn't notice. She asked, "How was school today?" but did not give him time to answer. This, in itself, is not necessarily a big problem, as all parents do it sometimes. But overall, Cameron's parents fail to notice his feelings, leaving him all on his own to manage and cope, and learn from his mistakes.

Cameron, Olive and Oscar, as a group, are lacking self-compassion. It's no one's fault, and no one asked for it. But sadly, it is the primary source of, and fuel for, Cameron's anxiety. And if Olive and Oscar had not done the excellent work they did soon after this event in couples therapy, Cameron would have grown up, married and had children, and unwittingly transferred this painful lack of self-compassion on to his own children.

3. Emptiness

Cindy, 26

It's 10 p.m. on a Thursday night, and Cindy is locking up the jewelry store, where she is night manager. Having just said goodnight to the salesperson, she is alone in the store for a moment. She begins to think ahead, to her 15-minute drive home to her apartment. Picking up her phone, she texts her best friend and roommate Trish, "Home in 15. Do something?"

Driving home, she listens for a response from Trish, but hears no text alert. After parking her car, she checks her phone to make sure there was no response, and confirms that is the case. "I wonder where Trish is. I hope someone is home," she thinks, dreading the idea of walking into an empty apartment.

To Cindy's chagrin, however, the apartment is indeed unoccupied. "Well, no problem," she thinks. "I can use some alone time. I'll make myself some spaghetti, and someone will be home soon, I'm sure." A little bit later, after finishing her pasta and watching a show on Netflix, the silence of the rooms weighs down on her. The aloneness burns through her chest, leaving her feeling empty and hollow. She checks her phone again. Nothing. "This is ridiculous! Why would Trish completely ignore my texts? This is so unlike her! I guess she completely forgot that I exist tonight." This thought replaces some of the hollowness in her chest with anger at Trish, but it also drives her more deeply into a severe "alone" feeling.

Cindy knows this feeling well, as it has been a frequent companion since she left home for college seven years ago. She "knows" the feeling, but she is not aware of it. She has instead learned to cope with it in her own way. Each time Cindy feels this hollow longing in her chest, she takes action, and this time is no exception. "Where are those cinnamon rolls someone left here the other day? I know they're here somewhere," she vows as she begins to rifle through the cabinets.

Do you recognize the hollow, empty feeling Cindy experiences? She feels this emptiness mostly for the same reasons that you do. Cindy is a self-contained, self-sufficient, independent young woman. She is also bright, resourceful and, in many ways, uncommonly strong. But she has one tremendous weakness that is her Achilles heel. Her strong framework is built upon shifting sands. She must work hard to manage those sands, and lives in fear that her framework will collapse.

Cindy's shifting sands are, of course, her emotions. She has many every single day, and she had many during her childhood and adolescence. She had layers of deep feelings during her father's cancer scare, and she has done the same with every one.

As you recall, Cindy was raised by Oscar and Olive, who were, throughout the decades of parenting their children, blind to their own emotions as well as to hers and her brother Cameron's. As a result, Cindy's feelings went unnoticed and under-responded to in her childhood home. Cindy did not learn the language of emotion growing up, nor did she learn to identify her feelings, tolerate or use them. From this, she absorbed that powerful CEN message with which we are all so familiar: *your feelings don't matter.* Cindy learned early and well how to escape her feelings rather than accept and use them. Cindy is now living without a vital, rich resource that others enjoy: her emotions.

Fortunately for Cindy, help is on the way, because her parents have done a remarkable thing. They have gone far toward healing their own Childhood Emotional Neglect, and soon they will reach out to her, offer her their hands, and encourage her down the path of recovery with them.

4. Inaccurate Self-Appraisal

Cameron, 17

It's a beautiful late summer day, and Cameron is walking, laughing and talking with a group of friends, heading toward the soccer field for the first practice of the school year. He is excited to demonstrate the passing skills he's been working on all summer, and he has high hopes for making the school's varsity team this year.

The coach gives the players a little speech about how try-outs will go this year, and explains that today is only a warm-up. "I want you all to relax, do the drills, and focus on where you need to improve. I'll be watching, and getting an idea of how to help each of you maximize your skills. Somewhere, out of this group of about 80 players, I will be choosing my 30 top players for the varsity and junior varsity teams. Now let's get this thing going!"

The coach's announcement is greeted with a loud cheer from all the players as they disperse into their skill drills. Cameron works his way through the dribbling, turning, crossing and heading drills, and finally arrives at the passing drills. Out of the corner of his eye, he sees his coach is watching him. "He knows this was my weak point last year. He is going to be amazed," he muses. Running alongside the ball, he expertly passes it to a teammate, and then turns around to watch the other players' passes. With a sinking heart, he sees that his teammates have also been practicing over the summer, and have grown larger and stronger too, and that they have already outshone him.

At the end of practice, Cameron feels like the coach has barely noticed him or his improved passing skills. With his friends talking animatedly around him and high-fiving each other for having completed the first practice of the season, Cameron slinks quietly in the direction of home, hoping that no one catches up to him. In his head, he is thinking this: "Why do you even bother to try? You'll never make first string. You're just not athletic, and you need to face it."

Given Cameron's prior experience on his chemistry test, you are probably not surprised to learn of his reaction to the soccer practice. But here, we are looking at a different facet of the Emotional Neglect he has grown up with. In this instance, Cameron is not only showing a lack of self-compassion, he is showing a lack of something even more broad and essential, self-knowledge. And his lack of self-knowledge is costing him dearly, making him less resilient to challenge, and more prone to giving up.

The truth is, Cameron is in fact very athletic. He can move quickly on his feet and has excellent hand-eye coordination. And he does, at times, have an awareness of these skills within himself. But his awareness is fragile because he has gained it from moments and people outside of his childhood home. Cameron has seen his coach's eyes light up when he's scored a goal with particular skill. He has been told by his friends that they are envious of his quick feet. His parents have been to a number of his soccer games, and always give him generalized comments about how well he played (even if he didn't). But they have sadly failed to do what really matters. They have not given him specific feedback about what they've noticed about his passion for soccer or about his strengths and weaknesses as an athlete, as a student, or as a human being.

Throughout Cameron's soccer career, for example, his parents have not noticed that he's been upset with himself about his passing skills, and they did not notice that he spent hours perfecting that skill over the summer. They have not said to Cam enough things like, "You are a committed member of the soccer team, and it's so neat that you always do whatever it takes to better yourself." They missed the fact that his amazing hand/eye coordination and quick feet were his greatest athletic strength.

Instead of knowing exactly who he is and what he's good at, Cameron is left to try to figure it out on his own. He's confused about his own athletic skills, strengths and weaknesses, so he has nothing to fall back on when things don't go as he expects. Because of the lack of specific, realistic, uncritical, essential feedback from his parents, he struggles to see himself clearly in every area of his life.

Imagine if Cameron knew about his special abilities with speed and hand-eye coordination, and fully owned those skills because his parents had reflected them back to him. Imagine if he had a fund of knowledge about his own passions, motivations, personal qualities, and personal challenges. Imagine if, when he found that his passing practice over the summer left him still falling short among his competitors, he was able to conclude, "I always knew passing would be my weak spot. I'm going to keep working on it, and I'm also going to use my superior speed to make up for it."

That would be the kind of resilience that every parent wants his child to have. That would be the kind of resilience that can only come from having a clear and accurate picture of one's self. That is the kind of self-knowledge that one can get from having parents who are truly watching, and lovingly feeding their observations back to him.

Parent Responsibility Check: Remember that no parents are able to observe every small detail about their children, and I don't mean to suggest that anything less than that will leave the child with CEN. The problem for Cameron is not hinging on this one specific failure of his parents to notice his exact athletic strengths and weaknesses. His parents, Oscar and Olive, were each raised themselves by parents who were not looking at them, and did not see their true nature. They managed to deliver far more individual attention to Cameron and Cindy than they received in their own childhoods. But they were not able to deliver fully to their children the rich, layered, multi-faceted, comprehensive observations that only an emotionally attuned parent can give.

They were not able to give what they did not have. It wasn't their fault.

5. Guilt and Shame

Martha, 6

Martha plays in her family room with her two favorite friends, Simon and Lara. They are taking turns hitting and pitching, using a big plastic bat and Wiffle ball. Simon and Lara are serious about the game and are keeping score. Martha, on the other hand, is feeling bored with this game, and is lapsing into silliness.

"It's your turn to pitch to me," Simon says to Martha. "Try to aim right this time." Martha picks up the ball and tosses it behind her head in a high arc while saying in a silly voice, "Yes, whatever Simon says," and then falls on the floor laughing. Simon and Lara exchange annoyed glances, and Lara says, "Seriously, Martha, play right. We need to finish this game!"

Realizing her friends are getting frustrated, Martha picks up the ball and does her best to pitch it properly. Unfortunately, truly by accident, it veers off to the left, missing the base by over a foot. "OK, that's it. You're out of the game," Simon declares. He picks up the Wiffle ball and tells Martha that he and Lara are going to finish the game on their own. Standing to the side, Martha watches her two friends play without her, continuing to keep score. Eventually, she plops on the couch and watches, while a wave of emotion creeps from her belly into her chest, growing ever more intense. Feeling angry, rejected, and excluded by her best friends in her own home, she finally stalks over to Lara and, grabbing the bat out of her hands, she starts walking out of the room with it.

Busy working in the kitchen, May hears loud protests and yelling, and immediately heads toward the family room. Seeing her daughter leaving with the bat and hearing her friends' protests, May thinks to herself, "Here we go again. When will Martha learn?" Removing the bat from Martha's hands and returning it to Lara, May pulls Martha into the next room and closes the door.

"Martha, this is unacceptable. Sit here until you've calmed down,"
she instructs, and leaves the room, closing the door behind her.

Sitting in a pool of misery, her sobs rising in her throat,
Martha feels it all. Anger, frustration, rejection, hurt, unfairness,
all surrounded by a thick cloak of shame. "What is wrong with
me?" she desperately asks the empty room, straining her six-year-
old mind for an answer.

In this situation you can see that little Martha has experienced a great deal of complex and varied emotion. But there are also multiple layers of feelings involved here, and they are very important to understand. Martha is feeling the pain of her friends' unfair treatment and exclusion of her. On top of that, she feels misunderstood by her mother, who appears to be automatically taking her friends' side. She feels targeted and mistreated.

But here is the most important of all the feelings Martha is having. Martha's mom's reaction to this situation is resulting from Martha's previous emotionality. She is known for her emotional reactions, which her mother and other adults have referred to as "fits" or "tantrums." She knows that her parents want these to stop, and she also wants to stop them herself, but she simply doesn't know how to do so.

No adult in Martha's life is talking with her about any of these complex feelings that she's having. Instead, they are responding to her feelings with exasperation, frustration, and labeling. No one is shaming her for her feelings, but no one is validating them either. Martha is not learning what she needs to know about how to understand, tolerate or express her feelings or emotional needs.

That's why deep underneath all the feelings she is having at this moment runs a powerful river of guilt and shame. She feels guilty that she is crying, and ashamed that she is feeling. Her little brain is making a powerful, damaging connection that no one knows about, and no one wants her to have. Her brain is coupling emotion with guilt and shame, and this is setting her up to have them coupled in her mind for a lifetime.

When she feels emotion, she will automatically feel ashamed. This experience is so unpleasant for her that, together with a lack of emotion vocabulary and emotion skills, she will naturally push her feelings down and away so that she can stop being a problem for her parents, and so she can stop feeling ashamed.

That is the natural process of Childhood Emotional Neglect. Six-year-old Martha, whose parents love and care about her, but whose mother never had the opportunity to learn about emotions, is well on her way to a lifetime of CEN.

6. Anger and Blame

Michael, 11

At age eleven, Michael is May and Marcel's oldest child, and a caring older brother to Martha. Michael's nature is quite different from his little sister's. He is a calm, quiet child. When Martha becomes emotional, Michael has learned to be as quiet as possible and to stay out of the way so that his parents can handle it.

On this day, Michael's parents have told him and his sister that they need to talk with them both about something important. "Come on into the kitchen, kiddos, we need to share something with you," they say. Michael distractedly puts his football down on the porch and follows Martha into the kitchen.

"We have to tell you something that we know is going to be disappointing for you," his father says. After exchanging glances with May, Marcel says, "It looks like we're not going to be able to go to the giant waterpark in Florida over school break next month after all." Marcel tries to continue to explain, but Martha's reaction prevents it.

"Noooooooo," she yells loudly, tears already running down her cheeks. "We ARE going! You said we're going and we ARE going!"

"Calm down, Martha, and let Dad explain," May says to her daughter. Marcel walks up and puts his hand on Martha's *shoulder, trying to quiet her. "I'm so sorry, kids," Marcel says, "but it turns out that I'm going to have to work through school vacation week. I tried so hard to get out of it, but there's just no way. I promise you we will go either during December break or next spring." Marcel barely finishes talking before Martha, realizing the futility of the situation, falls into loud sobs." She runs out of the room, and Marcel follows her.*

May now turns her attention to Michael, who is sitting quietly, looking sad. "Thank goodness you are so calm, Michael. I don't know what we would do if you got as upset about things as your sister does." Feeling somewhat complimented, Michael does his best to put on an expression that conveys to his mother that he is fine. "Can I go back out and play now?"

"Sure, sweetie," May says, opening the door for Michael and tousling his hair a bit as he goes through it. As Michael picks up his football and walks toward the street to find his friend, he is feeling intensely. Deep disappointment and anger swirl and percolate and threaten to erupt. But Michael has no idea what these feelings are, or what to do with them. Breaking away from the path to his friend's house, he starts walking in circles aimlessly, tossing the football up in the air while he tries to get his emotions under control.

Instead, tears begin to leak out and run down his cheeks. "Nothing ever goes right for me," he thinks. "It's like I'm hexed or something. I'll probably never, ever, ever get to go to that waterpark."

As you can see in this moment, Michael's well-meaning, loving parents have failed to respond to his feelings. Through no fault of their own, they have become caught up in Martha's more powerful, more obvious emotions, and have missed Michael's. Might this experience make Michael stronger? Perhaps, in a way. He is learning to control his feelings as needed, which makes him seem impervious and "calm." But he is also learning a toxic coping mechanism that will harm him over time. He's learning to turn his anger against himself instead of at its proper target (in this case, his parents and his father's boss). He is perceiving this letdown as an extension of himself and his own bad luck instead of an external, unpredictable, uncontrollable adult situation that has nothing to do with him.

Michael is learning to blame himself.

7. The Fatal Flaw

Cindy, 26

Cindy is busy restocking some shelves in the jewelry store when she hears her boss, Mary, come up behind her and unexpectedly say, "Cindy! You and I are going to a convention together next Tuesday."

"Oh. Cool, okay," Cindy stammers, feeling complimented that her boss is inviting her, since it's a sign that she is earmarked for a Day Manager position at the store. At the same time, though, Cindy's brain is scrambling to process and manage this new information. Somewhere, deep down, she is feeling a strong discomfort with this idea. The best word for this uncomfortable feeling would probably be "anxiety."

Unfortunately, Cindy is not consciously aware of this feeling. But her conscious mind does know that this is a good thing. So she focuses on the positive, and spends the next few days preparing herself for this conference experience by trying to whip up some enthusiasm about it.

On Tuesday, Cindy readies herself to walk into the conference and look for her boss. She is feeling that deep discomfort (anxiety) again, but compels herself through the large glass doors in something like a forced march. Entering into a large mass of people, she looks around for her boss but does not see her. "I'll get in line to register, and maybe she'll appear somewhere," Cindy thinks. Meanwhile, she looks around her and sees people chatting happily with each other, and walking in large groups. This makes her feel incredibly awkward, and conspicuously alone.

With her anxiety rising in her chest, she looks around for her boss, Mary, in an even more urgent way. Still no visual on Mary. Finally through the registration, Cindy walks into the auditorium for the first presentation, and sits in a seat that's surrounded by empty ones. Sitting and waiting for Mary to appear, she feels the emptiness of the seats surrounding her, and feels like she sticks out like a sore thumb, as someone who is all alone.

Any young adult might find her first professional conference intimidating, and may have some natural and healthy anxiety going into it. But in this story, we see Cindy having the classic experience of CEN's Fatal Flaw. As we know, Cindy has pushed her emotions down and away, since they were not acknowledged enough by her loving parents in her childhood home. Since Cindy is not emotionally available to herself, she is unfortunately not able to use or manage her own feelings in this situation.

When your emotions are pushed away, you are lacking an important source of lively warmth and connection with others. Looking around, as Cindy is, you feel that everyone else has some unnamed quality or ability that you inexplicably lack. All the other people seem to be living their lives in vivid color, while you are, in contrast, residing in a world that seems more black and white.

This is why Cindy feels so awkward in this professional and social situation that is new to her. She is using a large amount of energy trying to ensure that she appears a certain way, fully unaware that all she actually needs to present to others is her true self.

Deep down, Cindy senses she is missing something vital that others have. Since she feels different from everyone else, she experiences herself *on the outside,* no matter where she goes. Cindy does not know it, but she is the victim of her own Fatal Flaw.

8. Struggles with Self-Discipline

Michael, 11

> *Walking home from school slowly and lazily with his two neighbor friends, Michael is already thinking about the math homework he needs to do when he gets home. "Let's play some football in your backyard," his friend Barry says as they reach Michael's house first.*
>
> *"Yeah, go get your football and we'll meet you in the backyard," Michael's other friend Rick says, already heading toward the back of the house.*
>
> *"Wait, no not yet!" Michael calls to them. "I have to do my math homework and chores. Come back later, OK?" Disappointed, his friends reverse directions and head to their respective houses.*

I know what you're thinking. "Wow. What a responsible young man Michael is!" And you are right. What eleven-year-old boy bypasses playing with his friends to do his homework and chores first? And the answer is: only one with Michael's nature, growing up in an emotionally neglectful childhood home.

We've already established that Michael is a calm, cooperative child who tries not to need much support or care from his parents so that they can deal with his more emotionally challenging sister, Martha. Previously, we talked about how Michael tries to stay below the radar at home, and that he knows his lack of neediness pleases his mother. Michael doesn't realize it, but he is driven by *a need to not need anything*. He has learned, on some deep unconscious level that was never intended by his parents, that he must not cause problems if he wants to feel loved, accepted and special.

So Michael tries to anticipate everything that his mother would ask him to do, and to do it before she needs to ask him. In many ways, this is working fine for him so far, but if it is left unchecked, it will become a serious problem when Michael goes away to college, and all throughout his adulthood.

Unfortunately, no matter how self-disciplined Michael appears, from this childhood set-up he is not learning self-discipline. Instead, he is learning how to have no needs. He has developed for himself, inside, the parental voice that he is managing to escape from the outside. His internal voice reminds him to do his homework or clean up his room. And like most children's internal disciplinary voices, Michael's is harsh when he makes a mistake.

Unfortunately, when Michael is older and living away from his childhood home, his need to do everything before his mother has to ask will no longer motivate him. As an adult, he will take forward the harsh voice he created as a child, and he will struggle to use that voice effectively to help him do things he doesn't want to do, or stop himself from doing things he shouldn't do.

As an adult, when Michael needs to make himself do something that's boring or difficult or tedious, his harsh child's voice will step in to push him. Then it will berate and shame him when he struggles or fails. Sometimes, in an effort to avoid that feeling of shame, he will simply not try, and may instead let himself off the hook altogether.

As a child, no parent is providing Michael with external structure in a firm but loving, compassionate way. No parent is talking him through his mistakes and failures so that he can hear the voice of Compassionate Accountability and internalize it. So Michael will not have this voice when he grows up.

Chances are high that Michael will someday be very puzzled by his struggle with self-discipline, especially since he has no memories of what he didn't get. He will look back at his childhood, and remember his loving and caring family. Most likely, he will see himself as the source of all of these problems. "Am I weak?" he will wonder. "What is wrong with me?"

9. Difficulty Nurturing Self and Others

Cindy, 26

Feeling a heavy weight pressing on her chest, Cindy drives toward the hospital where her father will soon be coming out of surgery. Her mother has asked her to arrive at around 3:00 so she can be there for the doctor's report. The biggest question of the day is whether they were able to get all the cancer in this surgery, or has the cancer metastasized. The answer will have profound implications on the future of the life of her father and her family.

Pulling into the hospital's parking garage, Cindy begins to tremble. Tears spring to her cheeks, and loud sobs escape her lips. Grabbing tissues quickly, she tries to wipe away her pain and fear. For some minutes she has no choice but to sit in her car and try to pull herself together. Finally, after some time, she gathers her belongings and hurries into the building, realizing that she is now late.

When Cindy sees her mother sitting across the lobby, she walks quickly toward her while struggling to erase the anxiety from her face. "I'm sorry I'm late, Mom, I got held up at…" she stammers, trying to offer an explanation.

"It's okay, Cindy. Your dad is out of surgery, and the doctors say they think he's going to be fine. They got it all." Stopping slightly short of reaching her mother, Cindy needs to dissolve into tears, and fall into her mother's arms. But instead, remaining at arm's length, she says rather stiffly, "Oh. Geez. That's awesome. I'm so glad."

Breaking this moment of awkwardness, Olive takes a step toward her daughter and embraces her. "See, I told you everything would be fine," she says.

In this story, we are seeing how the internal barrier that's built by Emotional Neglect keeps us separate from our own emotions, but also from the people we care about the most. When you are uncomfortable with your own feelings, you are also uncomfortable allowing other people to see them.

Cindy is not fully aware of the emotions she is having as she drives to the hospital, and she doesn't accept and process them. Instead, she battles them back and tries to hide them from her mother, and invents a story to explain her lateness.

In this frightening, intrinsically emotional situation, Cindy can't share her feelings with her own mother, and Olive cannot share her feelings with her daughter. They are each blocked from themselves, so they are blocked from each other. It's as if there's an invisible, unacknowledged rulebook in the family that dictates:

Don't talk about anything important.
Don't let anyone see your feelings.
Keep your emotions in check, at all costs.

Even in this frightening experience, Cindy and Olive cannot throw away the family rulebook. It governs them and blocks them, no matter what.

10. Alexithymia (Low Emotional Intelligence)

Cindy, Cameron, Michael and Martha

Of all the effects of growing up emotionally neglected, the one with the greatest impact and farthest reach is alexithymia. When your emotions are not addressed enough in childhood, your emotions are pushed away in adulthood. Throughout the most formative decades of your life, you are missing the opportunity to learn how emotions work. Which emotion is which? What do you do with an emotion? How are your emotions affecting your decisions? How do other people's emotions affect their behavior?

The effects of this lack of knowledge upon every single area of the emotionally neglected person's life could be compared to a severe disability or a missing limb. For this reason, we have already seen its effects on each of our four lovely CEN children as we've looked in on their lives. Now, let's go back to the scenes we've already talked about, and view them with a specific focus on the alexithymia that's inextricably woven into them.

Cindy, 26

As Cindy drove to the hospital during her father's surgery, she was taken by surprise, and overwhelmed, by her own feelings. Of course, this can happen to anyone at certain times. But here it happens to Cindy because she had not considered the intense challenge of this situation for her. Since Cindy does not know how emotions work, she didn't know to expect it to be painful or difficult so that she could thoroughly prepare herself.

The emotionally neglected sometimes walk through their lives almost like an automaton. Cindy will go where she's asked to go, and she will do what others need her to do. And she will do it willingly because she is a good and caring person. But in difficult situations, she's unable to thoroughly grasp the emotional layers, nuances and needs involved. For example, on her way to the hospital she didn't thoroughly understand the depth of her mother's need for her to be there when the doctors came out. Since she doesn't understand her own emotional needs, she won't be prepared for the fear, the anxiety, or the intensity of the relief that she will feel when she's at the hospital. Cindy is at the mercy of her own feelings, and is set up to struggle to understand herself, and others, for a lifetime.

Cameron, 17

Remember when Cameron became anxious during his chemistry test, lost track of time, and was fighting off tears by the time he arrived home? Remember how he avoided his friends afterward, and rushed home alone?

Unfortunately, all of those things happened because of, or were made worse by, Cam's alexithymia. If Cam were more aware of his own feelings and tendencies, he might have been able to anticipate that he would have some anxiety on a difficult chemistry test. He might have known to prepare himself for the challenge. After the test, Cam rushed home alone because he didn't know that a far better way to handle his bad test experience (and the anxiety and disappointment that resulted) would be to be with his friends, and perhaps tell them about it.

Cam doesn't understand the value of sharing bothersome things or painful emotions. This is why he hides them, and pushes them down whenever they arise. Cam has not had the opportunity to learn how to predict what he might feel, prepare himself emotionally for difficult situations, or manage his feelings in a healthy way. This is why he is at a disadvantage to those around him. This is why he is at the mercy of his inner self.

Michael, 11

As we saw from his internal reaction to the cancelled vacation to the waterpark, calm and quiet Michael has all of the same emotions as any other healthy child. However, since he believes that keeping them hidden is his duty, he isn't able to learn how to name, express, understand or use his emotions.

Even now, as a child, Michael's lack of emotional education affects him. Lacking an outlet for healthy emotional processing, Michael often feels confused about what is going on in his world. Sometimes, in watching other children interact with their siblings and parents, Michael feels a yearning he can't understand. At other times, when his emotionally connected father, Marcel, is leaving on a work trip, Michael tries to avoid saying goodbye for fear that he may cry uncontrollably. This, he does not understand.

Because Michael's father is emotionally connected (you might recall that he did not grow up with CEN), Michael does have some level of emotional education in his life. But he is sometimes confused by the differing responses he receives from his father versus his mother.

We would not expect an eleven-year-old child to have a sophisticated understanding of emotions, of course. But Michael at this age is more at sea than other children, who are learning. If this is not changed, Michael will grow up to have his own version of Cindy's and Cam's struggles. He will be living in a confused world, separated from and puzzled by his own emotions and the emotions of others. He will be living with alexithymia.

Martha, 6

As we saw already, little Martha is learning that her emotions are excessive. Of course, we know that this is not true. Unfortunately, other than this false notion, Martha is learning little else about emotion.

A bright child, Martha will learn to smooth over her strong feelings as she grows. She will figure out some aspects of how emotions work. She shows signs of these progressions already in that she manages her emotions well when she is at school, and also does so better when her father is around.

Martha will benefit from the emotional responsiveness she gets from her dad. Like her brother Michael, even if nothing changes in her family, she won't grow up completely devoid of emotional understanding and awareness. But she will, unfortunately, have a much greater mountain to climb in this respect than other children will.

As she grows up, Martha will feel afraid of, and deeply uncomfortable with, strong emotion, whether it comes from others or she experiences it within herself. She will probably use avoidance as a primary coping technique. She will struggle to understand her own behavior, and will be puzzled by other people's actions as well. Overall, no matter how bright Martha is, she will be operating at a disadvantage in this world, all because of her alexithymia.

Summary

We have now covered the struggles of the CEN adult, parent and child. I hope that while reading it you were identifying with some of these lovely people, and that you were realizing you are not alone. I also want to make sure that you come away from these last two chapters with plenty of hope.

For there is plenty of hope for Marcel and May, Oscar and Olive, and Cindy, Cameron, Michael and Martha. Indeed, as you read on you will see that both of these families make a courageous choice to get themselves on a healthy, emotionally rich and connected track. You will see how they do it, and you will see that you can do it too.

The thing about Childhood Emotional Neglect is that it lays like a wet blanket over your life when you're living it, unknown. But it also offers a powerful path to connection, purpose and fulfillment when you see it and address it. Parents can heal themselves, and reach out in a new way to their children.

Read on, because this is what all of our CEN people are about to do.

Chapter 13

CHANGING YOUR PARENTING STYLE

❝ *Human babies are born with parental emotional sonar.* **❞**

In this chapter, we will be covering a substantial amount of information about how you can enrich and repair your relationship with your children. Whether your children are very young, teenagers, or adults with lives and families of their own, I want you to know that it's never too late to begin the repair process with them. It's never too late to make positive changes that will make your connection healthier and richer and deeper. As I've already mentioned several times in this book, you can heal your own CEN, and now we're going to talk about what you can do to help your children onto the healing path too.

One of the most important things you can do as a parent is identify your own emotional blind spots, and start filling them. In truth, this is the most deeply profound thing that you can do to change your children's lives. Being able to see yourself, know yourself, respond to your own needs, and accept emotional support from others makes it possible for you to see your child, know who she is, respond to her needs, and provide her with emotional support.

Human babies are born with parental emotional sonar. No matter your children's ages, they are ultrasensitive to your feelings, needs, choices and actions. Imagine that your son or daughter is 5, 12, 16 or 47 years old. Imagine him or her watching you begin to behave in a way that is uncharacteristic of you. He sees you express something that you need or want, ask for help and accept it, or express your feelings about something assertively and unapologetically. Since your child's brain is wired by nature to yours, he will, on some level, be affected. Even if he does not consciously take note of the change, he will absorb it, and it will, ever so slightly (or perhaps even more) change him.

There are three significant changes you can make today in your interactions with your children, despite their ages, that will deliver a powerful healing effect between you. To maximally accomplish these, it will be helpful to keep working on healing your own CEN, of course. But you can begin making these three changes immediately. Afterward, we will talk about specific ways, based on your child's age, to deepen your relationship. And then, in the next chapter we will talk about whether you should talk about CEN with your child and, if so, how to go about it.

Three Changes You Can Make Now with Children of Any Age

1. Talk More

As parents, we know our kids, and they know us. Over time, it's natural for our relationships with them to become routine and based on mutual understanding rather than communication. It's easy to coast along, interacting with each other mostly on an as-needed basis. That's not necessarily a bad thing, but it is definitely not a way to prevent or heal CEN. Consider how much you talk with your children. How many words are exchanged? I'm not encouraging you to talk at them or bore them with meaningless conversation, but to instead set your mind to communicating more with them in general. Share more with your child about yourself, your views, and what matters to you. Ask your child more about herself, her views, and what matters to her. Increasing the word count between you, when done with purpose and care, will also increase the mutual understanding. Also, when you talk with your child, you are automatically communicating that she matters to you.

2. Get More Curious / Ask More Questions

By this I mean become more interested in what's going on in your child's life and in her head. What's she worried about, what's she thinking about, what's she happy about, how are things going? Instead of absently asking, "How was school (or work) today?" which allows for an empty answer like "Good," ask something more specific. Ask her what she did today. Ask her to tell you a story about her day. Follow up on something specific that you talked about before. "What ever happened with that friend you had the argument with?" for example. If your child is a teen or if your relationship is in need of repair, your questions may be rebuffed. That's okay. Remember that receiving a meaningful answer is a bonus, but just as with talking more, every time you ask your child a question, you are telling her, "You matter to me. I'm interested." And that is a worthwhile accomplishment in itself.

3. Use More Emotion Words

Here, we are trying to increase your child's awareness of emotions in general, his own as well as the emotions of others. Using more emotion words is a way to increase your child's emotional vocabulary (for this, it helps to use a rich variety of emotion words if you can). Imagine the difference between saying, "Wow, you must be tired," and "Wow, you must feel overwhelmed and depleted." Or imagine instead of saying, "I'm worried about getting my passport in time," you said, "I'm feeling anxious and helpless about getting my passport in time." The second example of each shows a level of awareness of your own and your child's inner experience that's slightly more nuanced and meaningful. Using more feeling words also normalizes and legitimizes feeling talk, communicating to your child that what she is feeling matters to you, that your own feelings matter to you, and that you want to have more meaningful exchanges (and thereby a more meaningful relationship) with her.

How to Prevent CEN and Enrich Your Relationship with Your Small Child

Although the three general guidelines above work for children of all ages, we also need to consider more specific ways that you can work with your own children that take their developmental stages into account. First we will talk about pre-adolescents, then adolescents/teens, and finally adults. Even if your children are older, I hope you will read through the suggestions for younger children, since some will apply to older children as well, including adults. That's because when it comes to preventing and healing CEN, much of the solution comes down to variations on one simple theme: validating and responding to emotions. You are the best judge of which efforts are likely to work best on your child.

1. **Treat your child in an age-appropriate manner.** This strategy may seem silly when you first read it, but I assure you it is not. One of the greatest challenges of parenting is that your child is always changing. I have seen many parents damage their emotional connection with their child by expecting more from the child than is natural for his age, or by babying the child. Small mistakes and adjustments are natural to the developmental process, of course. But when a parent fails to notice or respond to a child's natural growth and limitations on an ongoing basis, the message to the child is, "I don't see you. I don't know you." And the converse is also true. When you treat your child in an age-appropriate manner, you are saying, "I see you struggling, and it's okay. I see what you can do, and it's wonderful."

2. **Observe and take note of your child's unique nature.** This involves simply paying attention. What does she love? What does she dislike? Is she shy? Outgoing? Active? Passive? Funny? Serious? What makes her angry? What are her pet peeves? What

riles her? Soothes her? What does she need? What are her social challenges? Her emotional challenges? What are her natural strengths and weaknesses? The better you see your child, the more known she will feel. And feeling known is a vital piece of feeling valid.

3. **Feed your observations back to your child.** Most of what you observe when you follow strategy #2 is valuable information for your child to have. Be sure to share your observations in a nonjudgmental, uncritical and supportive way. Your goal is to communicate to your child, "Here's who you are, and when it's all added up to make a picture of you, it is a fine picture." This helps your child know herself in a realistic way, and this is the bedrock of self-esteem and resilience.

4. **Do not avoid conflict with your child.** Making your child upset or angry may feel wrong to you, but avoiding it is the primary trait of the Permissive Parent. Your child needs you to structure and discipline him so that he'll grow up able to structure and discipline himself. Unfortunately, some conflict between parent and child is built into the discipline process. When you go through that conflict with your child, enforcing rules and limits with firmness and love, and come out the other side of each incident with your love for each other intact, you are teaching your child how to structure, limit and discipline himself with firmness and love. You are teaching him Compassionate Accountability.

5. **Always keep in mind that emotions are powering your child's behavior.** When you react to what your child *does*, you are likely missing what she *feels*. Yet, in most cases, her actions are driven by her feelings. When you look beneath her behavior, and respond to her feelings, your child will feel that you care, and that you understand her. She will also learn some important information that will help her understand herself. So, while you are setting limits on your child's behavior, also think about (or

even ask her depending on her age and emotional vocabulary) what she is feeling. "Why are you doing that?" is often more fruitful than, "Stop doing that." A good rule of thumb is: First respond to the emotion, then respond to the behavior.

6. **Strive to feel your child's feelings.** This is empathy, and it's invaluable between you and your child. Every time you put yourself in your child's shoes and feel what he feels, you are communicating and connecting with him in the deepest, most meaningful way possible. "I feel what you feel," is the language of real love. True empathy is free from the strings and barriers of judgment. It has nothing to do with agreeing or endorsing or evaluating your child's feelings. Your child's emotions are not subject to these rules. You may set limits on behavior, but you will still always strive to feel his feelings. This will teach your child that his feelings are real and important, yet he still must answer for his behavior.

7. **Encourage your child to ask for what she needs and wants, and to express her preferences and wishes.** (Important note: This is not the same as always granting them.) You can do this simply by asking him. "Do you need help?" "Do you want salad?" "Do you like these shoes or those shoes?" "What color do you like best?" Encouraging your child to ask for things and express himself sets him up to know that his wishes, needs and preferences are important, and helps him feel comfortable expressing them throughout his lifetime.

8. **Share your own feelings with your child.** As you work on your own CEN, you are becoming more aware of your own feelings. As you do so, consider allowing your child to see more of them. It's important to carefully screen which emotions you share and how you share them, of course. But letting your child see that you are angry, sad, happy or hurt sometimes helps them see your humanity, and communicates to them that you're okay letting your true self show. If you can also carefully label what you are

feeling, this teaches him the language of emotion. Be sure to keep the feelings you're sharing under control, and be aware of your child's reactions to them. "I'm just a little frustrated right now, sweetie." "It's okay, hon, it's just that my feelings are kind of hurt." Combining your honest emotion with reassurance and candid sharing is a helpful emotional education for your child. A helpful guide to what to share is to ask yourself the question: Would I have wanted to hear this from my parent when I was my child's age? If you had little to no relationship with your own parents, this question may not be helpful to you, and that's okay. Just keeping in mind the goal to only share what is age-appropriate will serve you well.

9. **Speak the language of emotion with your child.** Although it must be possible to overdo this one, I don't think you should worry about that. It will be good for your child overall to know that you see what emotion she's having, because you're labeling it for her; that you know what emotion you're having, because you're saying it to her. Drawing her attention to the deeper side of life will give her an advantage to enjoy throughout her adolescence and adulthood. This is a building block for emotional intelligence, which has been shown by research to contribute greatly to life satisfaction and success (Urquijo, I., Extremera, N. and Villa, A, 2016).

10. **Don't expect your small child to use emotion words.** Most children don't, and it's OK. The more you share of yourself and put your feelings into words, the more your child will move toward doing the same as she grows. Talk, and your child will learn to talk. Share, and your child will learn to share. Show your feelings in a healthy, connecting way, and your child will learn how to do that as well.

11. **Follow the Three Steps of Parenting.** First, you feel an emotional connection with your child. Second, you pay attention to your child, recognizing that he is a separate person who may differ

greatly from you. And third, by using the emotional connection, and by paying attention, you respond competently to your child's emotional need.

Strategies for Adolescents

"Hi, son. It's just us, Mom and Dad. Remember? The shadowy figures on the periphery of your life. We just stopped by to say good night."

An old Italian proverb says: *Little children, headache. Big children, heartache.* If you have an adolescent, you understand this all too well. The separation process begins in adolescence, usually when you least expect it. The way you manage your own feelings, and respond to your child's feelings, during this complex and sometimes painful process matters very much. It will help lay the foundation for who your child will become, and will have a significant impact on the kind of relationship you will have with him in the future.

1. **Be aware of the intensity of your child's feelings.** Young children have intense emotions, but adolescents can feel even more intensely. Part of your job as parent is to help your child learn the role of those emotions in his life, and also how to manage them.

2. **Do not be afraid of your teen's emotions.** Teens can deliver powerful blasts of feeling, especially toward their parents. It's important to realize that what your adolescent is blasting is nothing more or less than feelings. Letting yourself become overly hurt, angered, or thrown off your game by this can give your child's feelings too much power. On the other hand, it's important to also acknowledge the feeling and its intensity. When your child displays intense emotions of any kind, try to respond to the emotion itself while also noticing the intensity, keeping in mind that teens often say things they mean in the moment, but not overall. For example, "I hate you," actually means "I feel like I hate you right now." To that, you can say, "I understand you're upset. I get it. I really do. But rules are rules, I'm sorry to say."

3. **Be aware that adolescents often try to hide their feelings.** An adolescent's emotional life is complicated by the fact that he is often highly motivated to hide his emotions. In fact, when a teen is going to great lengths to appear to *not* care about something, this can be taken as an indication of how very much he cares. Teens are quick to feel shame when their emotions are blatantly seen because it makes them feel vulnerable. So begin to be more careful about noticing and naming emotions when your child moves into adolescence. Even if you're just beginning to make changes in your parenting, you can respond to your adolescent' feelings without having to point them out. And when you do so, your teen will feel understood, and known. And validated.

4. **React to your child with empathy.** Strive to feel what your adolescent is feeling, whether it makes sense to you or not.

When you do, your teen will know it. Again, empathy happens independent of judgment, so never judge your teen for what she is feeling. Instead, hold her accountable for her actions.

5. **Teach your adolescent emotional balance.** The message you want to convey to your child is that his emotions matter, but they do not run the show. Emotions can and should be listened to, but they must also be managed. Every chance you get to walk with your child through an episode of emotion, name the feeling, discern its message, sort through whether an action is needed, and process how to manage that feeling, you are handing your adolescent an emotionally balanced future.

6. **Notice more about your child's moods.** Keep your eyes and ears open to your teen. Most adolescents are sometimes open to you, and sometimes closed for business. So try your best to be sensitive to his moods. By this, I mean when your teen is in a talkative or connected mood, put down whatever you are doing and take advantage of this open window. Conversely, don't try to talk to your teen too often when he's shut down (unless he's never open for business, in which case you have no choice). In general, keep a watchful eye as your teen naturally distances himself, so that he knows that you're still there, and you see him.

7. **Accept your teen for who she really is.** During the span of adolescence, your child will change dramatically. After all, she is in the process of becoming the adult she will one day be. One of the greatest risk factors for CEN is having a child whom you have little in common with, and your child's differentness is often accentuated by adolescence. As a human, it's hard not to judge your child for the ways in which she's different from you. At times, you're baffled by her feelings, her words, proclivities and choices. You may find yourself wishing she were different. When you find yourself here, BEWARE, for you have entered a dangerous area. Strive instead to accept who she is, while giving her the space to become. Adolescence is a time of practicing who

you want to be, so allow your child to do that. Accept, accept, and accept her some more. When you do, you will automatically validate, validate, and validate her more.

8. **Give your adolescent the space to make mistakes.** When you keep a watchful eye while also giving him space, you are conveying that you care, and also that you trust him. Allowing your teen to make wrong choices and experience the natural, real-world consequences is important training for life, *as long as you are watching, and always there to help him if he needs it.* If you're not watching enough as you give your child space, you are emotionally neglecting your child. If you're excessively controlling your child to prevent mistakes, you are also emotionally neglecting him.

9. **Have limits, and convey and enforce them.** Many, if not most, teens test limits at some point. By breaking your rules and laws to see what happens, they are assessing the seriousness of the rules and laws of the world at large. It's important to be clear about your rules, and to be predictable about your responses when your child breaks them. No matter how much your adolescent hates your rules, they will most likely become his own.

10. **Get to know your adolescent's friends.** It's very important never to do this in an intrusive way. But when you're driving a carpool, taking them for pizza, or when they're hanging out at your house, watch and listen. When it's appropriate, ask the friends natural questions about themselves. "Do you have any brothers or sisters?" "What are you planning to do this summer?" or "Which foreign language are you taking this year?" Never take up too much space with your teen's friends, but be friendly and interested, as appropriate. Err on the side of accepting them, even if you're uncertain, as this allows your teen to learn from his own choices and relationships.

11. **Never let the bond break.** Your teen is pushing away in a natural attempt to grow into his own. Here, you are called

upon to assist him in the most unnatural-feeling, challenging task that any parent has, letting him go. But what you must be extraordinarily careful to never do, is allow the bond between you to break completely. Because if this happens, it may be very difficult to ever get him back. So walk that delicate tightrope, giving him space while watching, setting reasonable limits with love, and accepting his true self. And never let completely go, no matter what.

Strategies for Your Adult Child

Your children are your children, regardless of their ages. Once your children are grown, it's difficult not to look back with some regret, and see the many things you wish you'd done differently. Of course, unfortunately, none of us gets a do-over. But the good news is that even once your parenting is finished, your relationship with your child is never done. Your relationship now continues to be a living, evolving connection that can and will change over time, and you can use this to your advantage by actively changing how you are with your child.

1. **Reach out to your child more.** If you see your child every day, then this may mean talking more. If your child lives some distance away, then reach out to her in other ways. Start calling her slightly more often. Use more words when you're together. This may surprise your child, and that's okay. Your goal is not to annoy her, but to give her the message that she matters deeply to you. This also warms your child up to the notion that change is coming.

2. **Start speaking the language of emotion more.** Be conscious when you're interacting with your adult child that your goal is to use more emotion words, and to share a more emotion-friendly interchange. See the examples under the Young Children and Adolescent sections above to get ideas for how to do this.

3. **Treat your grandchildren the way you wish you had treated your child.** For this, you can use the parenting strategies for children and adolescents outlined in the other two sections. Be careful not to do this in a way that bypasses your child, as you don't want to convey that you care about your grandchildren's feelings more than your own child's (many grandparents make this terrible error). Be sure that you are also changing your emotional responsiveness to your adult child as you do this.

4. **Validate your child often.** It's never too late to notice your child's strengths, accomplishments, and lovable qualities. It's never too late to let your child know that you notice. There is not one tough forty-year-old man who would not benefit from hearing his parent say, "You amazed me when…" "I love how you are so…" "I can't believe what you accomplished, or how generous you are, or what a caring person you are." There are no limits to the ways that you can validate your child, and every time you do, you are emotionally strengthening him in a very real and valuable way.

5. **Share more of yourself with your child.** This strategy encompasses reaching out more, talking more, and sharing the language of emotion more. Tell your child some stories from your childhood. It's especially helpful if some of those stories have Childhood Emotional Neglect embedded in them, as Oscar's mother's did. Share more of your everyday life experience with your child, with a special goal of becoming more transparent, and more knowable on a deeper level to your child. When you do this, you are offering your child a path to a deeper connection with you.

6. **Strive for empathy.** Again, as I said in the other two sections, your empathy must be judgment-free. Try to feel what your child is feeling, whether you agree with it or not. This is even more helpful if there is some conflict in your relationship. When

you strive to feel your child's emotions, she will feel it. When you succeed, she will feel that too.

7. **Focus on connection, not conflict.** This requires you to put any longstanding conflicts aside, even if you can't let go of them. Remember that your parenting is done, but your relationship surely is not. You are still the parent in the relationship, so the responsibility for reaching out and connecting falls on you. Do your best to shift your focus away from the source of the conflict (unless it's so egregious that doing so would be enabling a damaging behavior or situation with your child) and toward connection. Conflicts between parent and child are much easier to solve when there is a feeling of reliable acceptance coming from the parent, and when there is an emotional connection in place.

8. **Ask more questions.** This is an easy and valuable way to communicate to your child that you are deeply interested in her. Ask her questions about her life, her work, her own parenting struggles. Listen carefully to her answers, and follow up later if it's a developing situation. The technique of vertical questioning works very well with adult children. Vertical questioning involves asking questions in a progressive way that helps the other person focus inward, taking them toward their own feelings. To use vertical questioning, ask questions like, "How did that feel?" "Why did you do that?" "What were you thinking right then?" as a way to help your child focus progressively inward during a conversation. This also takes you both away from the surface facts and logistics that can make a conversation feel shallow and meaningless.

9. **Consider talking with your adult child about CEN.** This can be the ultimate step toward healing your relationship with your child, but it's not indicated in every case. If you think it could be helpful to talk with your child about CEN, it's definitely a

good idea to begin warming up the connection between you by getting a good start on numbers 1-8.

Summary

Congratulations! Having read through the last several chapters, you have digested material that would have bypassed you only a few months or years ago, before you saw your CEN and began to understand what was missing in your life. I want to tell you that the fact you have read this intense and challenging information says some very important things about you as a person and a parent. You care about your children and their happiness and well-being, and you are willing to back up that care with action and effort. No matter what mistakes you have made as a parent, no matter what you've missed so far in your relationship with your child, you are, in the highest sense of the word, loving.

Whether your child is a toddler, teen or adult, you can make a significant impact on the CEN between you by working to implement all of the strategies we just talked about. To see how those changes look in real life, be sure to read Chapter 15: Portrait of Two Healing Families. There, you will learn exactly how Oscar and Olive and May and Marcel put the strategies into action with their children. And you will see exactly how it all turned out for them.

But first, if you're considering reaching out to your child to talk about CEN, let's spend a chapter helping you think about the potential value in doing that. Also, if you do decide to talk about it with your child, we'll discuss what you can do to maximize your success.

Chapter 14

SHOULD YOU TALK WITH YOUR CHILD ABOUT CEN? AND HOW TO DO IT

   "   *It's far easier to fix what's wrong in your relationship with your child once you've addressed what is missing.*   **"**

If your child is a pre-adolescent, there is obviously no point in talking with her about CEN. First, the concept will be far above her head. And second, it's simply not necessary. You can emotionally strengthen your child and your relationship with her with a combination of addressing your own CEN and beginning to parent her differently, using the guidelines above. No worries, you have plenty of time. If your child is ten or eleven, you may want to read this chapter anyway. There could come a time in the future, after your child has grown and matured a bit more, that you will wish to introduce this topic to her. Reading this now can give you a framework to hold in your mind that may help you to know if or when a time might be right in the future.

If your child is either an adolescent, a young adult, or a fully grown, independent, self-sufficient person, talking about CEN directly might bring you some wonderful advantages. In this chapter, we will talk about how to make the decision about addressing CEN directly with your child. We'll discuss the various possibilities that may arise for you if you do so. And we'll also cover the potential risks, as there surely are some.

As we noted above, CEN in a parent/child relationship can be addressed, and healed in many situations, without ever talking about CEN directly. Whether this is true in your case depends upon the age of your child, his temperament, the particular way the CEN has played out, and how much anger there is in your relationship. First, let's consider the potential advantages and disadvantages of bringing up this topic with your child.

The Potential Advantages and Disadvantages

The Potential Advantages

- **Committing a loving act:** Your child's outward response to your talking about CEN with him is less important than his inner response. Even if he appears to take it negatively (read more about that in the Disadvantages section), his inner self is feeling you reaching out to him. His inner self is feeling your love. As you know from Part 2 of this book, all humans' brains are wired to need their parents' love and emotional validation. So no matter what happens on the outside, when you talk with your child about CEN, you are automatically giving him the messaging that "I love you" and "Your feelings matter to me." And that is like giving him vitamins that are full of emotional health. This can simply never be the wrong thing to do.

- **Establishing a common language:** When you say the words, "Childhood Emotional Neglect" to your child, and talk about the concept using words like "emotional validation," "emotional connection," "failure to respond enough," and "emotion skills," you are creating a powerful communication tool between you. This shared language will make it easier for you both to heal your relationship.

- **Establishing a common understanding:** Talking about CEN directly establishes a shared realization of what went wrong in your son or daughter's childhood. This common understanding can be incredibly fruitful in the path toward healing. The potential benefits of this for your child and for your relationship with him are, in fact, so great that I'm not able to adequately address them here. You will get an increasingly deeper grasp of them as you read on, throughout this section and the next chapter.

- **Addressing the blame factor:** Whether your child is aware of these feelings or not, chances are high that she harbors a significant amount of blame in her heart. She grew up with at least some of her emotional needs frustrated, and that is, in her mind, your fault. (We know, of course, that you were born into the same emotional deficit that she was). The naming of the problem, and the awareness that CEN is an invisible malady that transfers automatically from one generation to the next essentially removes the blame factor. This opens a door between you and your child that may have otherwise remained mostly closed.

- **Reducing the anger:** First, let me say that the CEN folks I have seen in my office typically talk about their parents in very loving and appreciative terms. Yet they have a tendency to inexplicably snap at their parents, avoid their parents, and share little deeply personal information with them. Often, their anger is very real, but very underground. Talking about CEN gives your child's anger an explanation, a reason, and a justification that makes sense. Nothing reduces anger like validating it and taking accountability for its cause. And that is exactly what you are doing when you talk with your child about CEN.

- **Building empathy:** I know I keep talking about empathy, and there are multiple reasons for that. Here, I mention it because empathy is the fertilizer that nurtures everything good to grow faster and lusher. We want to have it in spades between you and your child. When you share your childhood CEN stories with your child, you are offering her a view of you through the CEN lens. She will begin to see you in a new way, as she realizes that you grew up without some essential nurturing and tools, just like she did. Hopefully, she will experience some pangs of the pain you felt as a child, and she will see and feel how it mirrors hers. This can forge a new, deep and compassionate bond between you that you can grow and build upon.

- **Offering tools to heal:** If your child opens himself up to the CEN concept, he is opening up to a whole new world. Once you reach him on this level, you can give him far more than an explanation for what's been wrong. You can ask him to read some articles about Emotional Neglect so that he can learn more, and begin to identify his own blind spots. He can start the exercises throughout the second half of *Running on Empty, Overcome Your Childhood Emotional Neglect*, and begin down his own path of healing. And what could feel better than seeing your own child begin to reverse what went wrong, and set it right?

The Potential Disadvantages

- **It could make things worse before they get better:** If your child has a fair amount of anger at you, having it validated by your description of CEN may cause her to be more angry initially, especially if she's an adolescent. This is, however, typically a temporary stage that will subside with your continual increased awareness, interest and presence. Some amount of patience and tolerance may be required from you.
- **Your child could use it against you:** It may take some time for a full understanding of CEN to sink in for your adolescent or adult child. If your child grasps only pieces at first, or if his anger gets in the way of applying the greater understanding in his relationship with you, he may end up distancing himself more for a time. The words "Emotional Neglect" can be used as an accusation by some. Again, this is usually only temporary, but it does require strength and tolerance on your part.

- **It could potentially devalue the parenting changes you are implementing:** When you begin to change the way you are relating with your child, as you gradually become warmer and more emotionally connected in your interactions, your child won't know why you're doing it, and may not even consciously notice your changes. But he will certainly feel the change. There is great value in your child experiencing your new style as natural, and on a feeling level. Jumping in to offer explanations and reasons for your warmer style by talking directly about CEN could, for some, diminish the potential effects. For this reason, it may make sense to hold off on explanations, to see if you can transform your relationship more organically first. There is no rush to talk about CEN. And timing matters, as we will talk about shortly.

"Tell me all about yourself."

I know that this is a lot to digest and think about. Please do keep in mind that there may be no right or wrong answer to the question, and I encourage you to make much of this decision with a combination of your gut and your brain. All best decisions are made when these two are used together. In fact, one very reasonable approach is to simply wait until talking with your child feels right.

Now let's go through a series of questions that I specially designed to help you think this through in a structured way. As you answer them, they will gradually help you develop some answers and some plans.

Five Questions to Help You Decide

1. **How has your child reacted to the changes you have made in your parenting so far?** This is one of the reasons I encouraged you to start parenting in more emotionally attentive and responsive ways before thinking about talking with your child about CEN. Your child's response to your changes can inform you.

    Can you see, or feel, a difference in your child? Is he warming up a bit? Talking more, calling more, sharing more, for example? If so, this is a very good sign. If your changes are working, keep making them, gradually increasing or intensifying to become more emotionally attuned, as long as your child continues to respond positively.

    If the process is going well, there is no real reason to rock the boat by talking about CEN, especially with an adolescent. If your child is an adult, and also with some later teens, however, there may be more to gain by talking about CEN, at the right time and in the right way.

    If your child shows no response at all to your changes, you may want to give it more time. Or you may want to bring up CEN if you feel it may open a door that's now closed. Keep in mind that teens are in the process of separating, so adolescence can be the most difficult time to try to draw your child closer.

2. **Is it possible that your child is more emotionally aware or emotionally intelligent than you are?** Think about it this way: your children have grown up in a different world than you did. Today, more than ever before, emotion and mindfulness and psychological awareness are written about, talked about and studied. Has your child had therapy, or been to a support group of any kind, or does he have a propensity to read self-help books? If so, your child may be ahead of you in terms of emotional awareness and/or emotional intelligence.

   If that is indeed the case, don't feel bad, be happy! This will work greatly in your favor in this process. First, because your child is probably already looking for answers, and now you have some to offer him. Second, because your child may already have some understanding and vocabulary that will make it easier to communicate with him about CEN.

   Generally, if your child is more psychologically mindful or insightful, your way may be already paved toward a CEN conversation.

3. **Would understanding the concept of CEN, and having the shared CEN vocabulary, help your child connect with you?** This is not necessarily a yes/no kind of question. It's a question to help you think about your particular relationship with your unique child. Imagine her having a full understanding of CEN. Is this likely to improve your relationship?

   One of the great advantages of talking about CEN that we talked about above is empathy. Would your particular child feel warmer and closer to you if she could see the world you grew up in, why you struggled to parent her emotionally, and that you now want to repair your relationship?

   Some folks do better with change when they understand what's going on. Your child may appreciate your efforts more if he knows that you're trying, and understands why. If this is the type of child you have, it may be one good reason to talk with your child about CEN.

4. **Is your child angry at you?** Because, as I'm sure you already realize, anger is a barrier that keeps you at a distance from your child. Some angry CEN children get even more angry when their CEN parents begin to show increased emotional attunement. They can experience their parent's attempts as insulting or intrusive, or as I have heard some say, "Too little, too late."

Sometimes, if your child is very angry, talking with him about CEN can break through the anger, and offer an olive branch, particularly if you make sure to acknowledge the pain that CEN has caused him.

But another, equally valid strategy is to simply refuse to allow your child to reject you. Instead, keep up the steady drumbeat of emotional attunement. If you are persistent and refuse to give up, the huge majority of children will eventually give in, and allow some connection to begin to grow.

5. **Does your child seem aware of her anger at you, or give you hints about the reasons for her anger?** As we know, CEN-based parent/child anger often comes out sideways. That's because it's very possible that, since CEN is so invisible, your child may be unaware of her anger. Or she may feel badly about herself for having it.

That said, however, most adolescent and adult children do give hints about the reasons for their anger, *even if they're not aware that they are angry.* These explanations will often pop out unexpectedly, to the surprise of everyone, including the child herself. So my suggestion to you is watch for these hints, catch them in the moment if you can, and respond differently than you usually do. This means asking her what she means, or simply validating what she says (even if you don't at all agree with it). This can be a very effective method of warming your angry child to become more open to the topic of CEN, and carries multiple other benefits as well.

I hope these questions have helped you think through your relationship with your child, his unique nature, and the way both of these factors interact with your decision about whether or not to bring up CEN directly with him. If you are at this point feeling that you may want to do so either now or sometime in the future, let's talk about the factors that are important for setting yourself (and your child) up for success.

Set Yourself Up for Success

First, get your boundaries in place. One of the biggest mistakes you can make when talking about CEN with your child is going into it with weak boundaries. By this I mean without having a clear sense of the line between you and your child. What's your job in this conversation, and what's his? If you feel overly responsible for doing your child's job, you can cause more problems. And this we do not want.

Think of your job as leading the proverbial horse to water. Think of your child's job as taking a drink. Be careful about crossing over from your job to actually trying to make your child absorb, accept or act upon the CEN concept. I encourage you to focus your efforts on presenting CEN to him in the best way that you can, and that's it. It will be your child's decision to make use of this information, discard it, or shelve it for later. Many, many, many children, especially adolescents, shelve it. They will choose to take it off the shelf when they are ready, as long as you don't push them in the interim.

Remember that you are not responsible for your child's decisions, nor can you make him listen or accept anything. All you can do is present the information. That's all. That's your boundary.

Second, set your expectations small. It's important to set your expectations at a realistic level. I don't want you to hope for a huge transformation from your first conversation. Instead, I would like you to go into this conversation with one small goal of your choice. Often the most effective approach is to imagine this process as a series of conversations, not just one. Patience is your friend, so envision this in steps.

Start by identifying your first step. Try to set it small and achievable. Some examples might be to use the phrase "Childhood Emotional Neglect" with your child. It might be to give your child a hint that you grew up in an emotionally barren home yourself. It might be to tell your child that you're trying to change, or to introduce the idea that you are realizing the importance of emotion. If your goal is to simply plant a seed that you can grow over time, then you are going into this well.

Third, choose your setting. Think about your best moments with your child. To help with this, you may want to go back to Chapter 9, Talking with Your Parents about CEN, and read how Oscar and Olive chose their settings to talk with their parents. Even though they are in a reverse situation (child talking to parent), the same way of thinking may help you in making your choices.

To briefly recap here, it's helpful to choose a time and place that usually feels the least stressed between you and your child. On a long car ride, after Sunday dinner, when your child picks up or drops off your grandchildren; it can be any time at all. As long as your child is at his most agreeable.

If you can't think of a time that feels right, then consider the possibility of structuring the talk. Would your child respond best if you make a point to tell him there's something you'd like to talk with him about? Or set up some alone time with him first, and then introduce the topic? There is no right/wrong about planning this. It's all based on nothing other than your best judgment.

Fourth, prepare possible intros. Think about this as possible ways to bring up a subject that's probably deeper, or more emotional, than you and your child would normally discuss. The setting is one way to pave the way, and using the right intro is another. Think about how you and your child normally relate, at your most positive. Is it through humor? Is it when your child is telling you about an accomplishment? Once you identify your best mode(s) of communication, think of an intro that works with it.

> *You and I joke a lot, which is great. But now can we talk about something serious for a minute?*
>
> *I don't tell you often enough how proud I am of you. In fact, I've been realizing lately that I've missed lots of other things too. Can I tell you some more about that?*
>
> *I understand why you're angry at me. I've been reading a book that's been helping me get it. Can I tell you about it?*

One very effective and very loving intro is to wait for your child to show a sign of CEN, and use it as a way to bring up CEN in a loving and caring way.

> *Sometimes I worry about whether you're paying enough attention to your own needs. I have the same problem, you know, and now I realize how I passed that on to you. Can I tell you about it?*
>
> *I wish I'd learned earlier in my life that it's okay to let people help me. Then I could have taught you better. I read a book about how things like that get passed down through generations.*

Next, gather your tools. Your best first (or second or third) step may be to get your child to read an article about CEN that you've specially chosen for him. Or perhaps even to read *Running on Empty: Overcome Your Childhood Emotional Neglect*. Before talking about CEN with your child, you may want to look through my website and PsychCentral.com blog to identify one or more articles that you think your child might relate to. Then, as you talk with your child, ask him to read it.

> *I read an article about why it's so hard for some people to pay attention to their own needs, and I'm 100% sure it's exactly about myself and you. If I email it, will you read it?*

Last but not least, take responsibility. Notice that the parent is taking care not to talk only about the child, but is instead talking about himself, and what he has passed on to his child. This is an important piece of your conversation. Be careful not to express your concern in a way that your child might take as criticism. Including yourself in your concerns is a way to take responsibility. By taking the "blame" for the problem, you're freeing him up to listen.

Summary

From reading this chapter, I hope you took several important messages. Talking about CEN with your child is a gesture of love. It may disrupt your relationship for a bit, but it will likely pay off in the long run. Have patience, choose your moment, and prepare.

If your child is angry, take this time to put all conflict aside. Because in bringing up CEN, you are slicing a path through all of the flotsam and jetsam of everyday life, and establishing a line directly from your parents, to you, and on to your child. That line goes back many generations, and has wreaked discontent, pain, and distance through decades of family relationships.

Conflicts and problems happen in every relationship, and some of your issues with your child may feel large and intense, and unrelated to CEN. But whether the problems feel large or small, shelving them temporarily so that you can talk about CEN is a remarkably healing step. Because, I assure you, it's far easier to fix what's wrong in your relationship with your child, once you have addressed what is missing.

Chapter 15

PORTRAIT OF TWO HEALING FAMILIES

May, Marcel, Michael and Martha

As you probably remember, Marcel discovered Childhood Emotional Neglect as the explanation for what was missing in his marriage. In an uncomfortable but loving conversation, he talked to May about it, and convinced her to read and learn about CEN. As May realized that she had grown up overshadowed by her mother's emotional needs, she, with Marcel's support, talked with her parents and set limits with them. She and Marcel came to couples therapy, and together we helped May get in touch with herself, become aware of her own feelings, and understand how emotions work and why they matter. During her CEN recovery process, May began paying attention to her own needs and her own self-care. She began to say "no" to the managing partners at work, assert her own wishes, and express her feelings to Marcel. Their marriage deepened, and together as a couple, they began to reap the rewards of May's hard work.

Not surprising to you, I'm sure, part of May and Marcel's recovery process included realizing the price that their children had paid at the hands of CEN. This was not easy for them to accept, but May used self-compassion and guilt management to stay strong and able to make the changes that were necessary to valiantly start giving her children what she never got from her own parents.

One day, as May was practicing emotionally attuned parenting by paying close attention to Martha's feelings and emotional needs, a realization about Martha began to crystallize in her head. "Martha has trouble with transitions," she thought. May also decided that since this information might be useful to her daughter, she should share it with her. And she knew the exact time that this information would be relevant and useful. That afternoon, she stopped by the school to pick up Martha, just like that day several months prior when Martha threw the fit that embarrassed her.

By now, though, in addition to setting some limits at work, May had begun practicing better self-care. As a result, she was feeling much less hurried, stressed and pressured as she walked from her car toward the playground where her children were. As she approached the group of children Martha was playing with, she could tell that Martha clearly saw her, as she made a dramatic turn so that her back was to her mother.

"Hi sweetie, I'm here," she called to her daughter, who quickly looked up and made a purposeful frownie face at her. Instead of becoming frustrated, as she had done before, May laughed lovingly at the face. "I know you're not ready, Hon. Ten minutes, okay Martha? Then we really do have to go."

"Five more minutes, Martha," May called to her daughter at the five-minute mark. Then, when it was time to leave, instead of announcing that, she asked Martha to come over to talk with her. Dragging her feet and looking upset, Martha obeyed. "Sweetie, I can see that you're in the middle of the game. Changing from one activity to another is hard for you, and I understand that." Martha appeared to be close to breaking down, but didn't. "I really

want to stay longer, Mom," she pleaded instead. "I know, I know, I know," May said. "I'm sorry, I know it's hard." Taking Martha's hand, she began to walk and talk. "When we get home, let's see if the glue is dry on that collage you and Lara made yesterday. If it is, where would you like to hang it?" Now interested in that prospect, Martha began to think about that as they walked over, hand in hand, to pick up Martha's backpack.

Several days later, Marcel came home from work and said, "Let's go out to dinner tonight! Where do you guys want to go?" Clearly happy about this idea, Martha got her vote in first. "The Spaghetti Shed, The Spaghetti Shed, The Spaghetti Shed!!" she shouted. May, careful to watch Michael's face closely, saw that he was looking unhappy with that idea, and was seriously considering his preference. "We went there last time," he said while watching Martha for any signs of an outburst. May watched Michael register some signs of anger in Martha's face, and she saw that he was going to tone down his own preferences to prevent an outburst. "I mean, their spaghetti's pretty good," he started.

"Michael, you want something else, don't you? I can see it," May said, drawing his eyes away from Martha and to her. "Don't worry about Martha, she's a big girl and she knows how taking turns works. Where do you want to go?" Heartened, but still a little nervous, Michael named his favorite Mexican restaurant.

"Nooooooo," began Martha in her classic style, but before she could get going, May walked up and hugged her tightly. "Little Bear loves spaghetti and sheds, and Little Bear knows that turns must be taken," she said in a silly voice, semi-quoting one of Martha's favorite books from when she was a toddler. Surprised by this difference in her mother, Martha didn't launch into screaming. Instead, she said, "I hate nachos," in a resigned voice. "Michael, will you help your sister pick out something different to try this time?" May said.

An outside observer would probably hardly notice any difference in May's parenting in these scenarios. But we do. We see that May has shown far more emotional openness to her children. She gave her children some valuable information about themselves. To Martha, she communicated that she has trouble with transitions, stated in age-appropriate words, "*Changing from one activity to another is hard for you.*" And she will repeat this in future situations to help Martha understand herself.

May communicated to Michael that she saw how concerned he was about not causing an outburst from his sister. "*Don't worry about Martha, she's a big girl...*" She gave him the reassurance he needed to assert himself, and she empowered him again by asking him to help his sister choose a new entrée.

Not all changes to emotional attunement go as smoothly as these. But there is something almost magical about seeing into your children's hearts, naming what they feel, and using it to teach them. Michael and Martha, at the ages of 11 and 6, are young enough to respond quickly to May's changes. They also enjoy the added benefit of a father who has been emotionally attuned all along.

Remember back to the beginning of this book, and our first portrait of Marcel and May. Remember how alone Marcel felt in his marriage, and how he felt the empty space between his wife and their children. Remember Martha's shame, and Michael's self-blame. Remember how puzzled May felt, as she tried in earnest to be a far better parent than her own mother, and could see that it still was not what her daughter needed.

On this beautiful late spring evening, driving home from the restaurant, May and Marcel stopped at the park to let Michael and Martha play. Sitting and watching the children, May leaning affectionately against him, Marcel bent to his wife's ear and whispered, "Thank you."

May looked into her husband's eyes, and knew exactly what he meant. She didn't need to say a thing.

On and on this family's lives move forward, joined together on a meaningful, emotional level, filling up all that old empty space with attunement and awareness, connection and understanding.

Truly, this is a family that is thriving.

Olive, Oscar, Cindy and Cameron

Olive and Oscar had come such a very long way. They had each faced down their own CEN, and they had deepened and repaired their marriage. As they both worked on self-awareness, self-care, and learning emotion and communication skills, they literally transformed their lives.

As these many changes were happening they, like Marcel and May, could see how their children had suffered as well. They had a teenage son having panic attacks at school and seemingly failing his most difficult class, and a young adult daughter who seemed angry, disengaged and distant. They knew that they had to change their ways of relating with their children. And fortunately, they knew how to do it.

Olive and Oscar started observing their son far more closely, with a special question in the back of their minds: "What is Cameron feeling right now?" They watched him when he got up in the morning, when he left for school, and when he came back, when he was leaving the house for soccer practice, and when he returned home. On weekends and weeknights, they paid attention. They also began to engage with him more.

When Oscar and Cam went on their annual fishing trip, Oscar shared with Cam some of what Cam's grandmother had shared with Oscar about her childhood. He made a few allusions to how that related to his own childhood (but did not connect it to Cam yet, as he was still in the early phases and didn't think Cam was ready).

In addition to noticing Cam's feelings, Olive began to engage with him on what she thought he was feeling. When Cam came home from soccer practice looking grim several days in a row, Olive said, "You look like you can use some iced tea. Hang on a minute while I pour you some." Then, while he was sitting on a chair at the kitchen table waiting, she said, "Are you still enjoying soccer as much as you used to? You don't always look all that happy when you come and go."

The first few times Olive asked Cameron questions like this, he either shrugged and walked away or seemed annoyed and said, "Don't worry about it, I'm fine." But Olive did not give up. She eased off when necessary, but continued to persist in simply paying more attention, and engaging more. Slowly, gradually, Olive and Oscar began to see some small differences in Cam. He was talking more to Olive, and told Oscar about his C on his chemistry exam, and then followed it up with, "I'm such an idiot, I studied the wrong stuff. I don't know what my problem is."

Oscar immediately saw the significance of what Cam had just shared. His immediate response was, "Whoa, Cam, hold on there, that's really harsh." Then, he asked to talk more with Cam about it later that evening, after he'd had a chance to think about it. He told Cam that he was bothered by what Cam had said, and asked if that's what goes on in Cam's head when he makes a mistake on a test. When Cam admitted that it was, Oscar gave Cam the phrase "Compassionate Accountability," and explained what it means. He shared that he had been overly harsh on himself for most of his life, and gave an example of how he had used Compassionate Accountability recently. Cam had seemed guarded at the beginning of the talk, but definitely listened and made a joke at the end that made it clear he had appreciated this conversation.

After the call several months ago from Cam's teacher about his anxiety attack, Olive and Oscar had held a meeting with Cam and his school counselor to discuss it. At that time, the counselor had explained to Cam that he had experienced an anxiety attack. The counselor had described it as the product of stress combined with a genetic predisposition, and asked them if anyone in the family had anxiety problems. Cam's parents had confirmed to the counselor that this was true but hadn't gone into it in any detail at that time.

With Cameron gradually warming to them, Olive and Oscar turned their attention to reaching out to Cindy. She would be more difficult in many ways, since she lived in the next state and was so emotionally removed from them. So they began putting much thought and energy into identifying small ways to reach out to her.

Cindy usually made her obligatory call to her parents about every other week. Her parents decided to shake up the pattern, and they began calling her every Sunday. At first Cindy didn't always answer. But after several months of regular, predictable calling on their part, she did begin to answer more often. Her more frequent answering may also have been encouraged by the nature of the calls themselves, as her parents were asking her more specific questions about her job, her friends and her life. They had no interest in jewelry, but asked her questions about it, and then listened carefully to her answers and followed up about them in the next phone call. They also began talking more meaningfully about themselves. Oscar shared some of the fear and anxiety he went through during his cancer surgery. They asked Cindy if they had shared enough with her and supported her enough through that difficult time. Cindy, of course, assured them that they had, but Oscar and Olive knew that was her CEN speaking, so they didn't take her answer as a complete truth.

Several times, when Cindy snapped irritably at her parents, Olive said in a loving and uncritical tone, "Cindy, what's that about?" Each time, Cindy seemed a bit embarrassed, paused for a minute and then said, "Nothing, Mom." But Olive could tell that she was becoming more aware that she was snapping, and that the snaps were affecting her parents.

Thanksgiving was coming, and Olive and Oscar decided to use this opportunity to shake things up some more with their two children. They explained to their two sets of parents that they needed to have some special conversations with their children this holiday, so would not be able to include them this year. Both sets of parents understood, since they were now aware of CEN and had talked about it with Oscar and Olive.

Olive called Cindy and asked if they could come to Providence where Cindy lived to have Thanksgiving there for a change. They added that they wanted some alone time for themselves as a family to celebrate Oscar's clean bill of health. Cindy seemed surprised, and readily agreed.

They had a fun and positive Thanksgiving weekend together as a family. No grandparents, no aunts and uncles, no family friends or neighbors. Just them. On Saturday night, they walked around downtown to look at the Christmas decorations together, and then went to a little restaurant for some dessert. It was there, at that moment, that Oscar felt it was finally time to bring up CEN to his children.

"Hey, guys, I have something I'd like to say. First, I want to make a toast to my good health. Second, I want to thank you, my two amazing children and my wonderful wife, for seeing me through that time. I don't know what I would have done if not for you guys, my favorite three people in the whole world."

Glancing around, he saw Olive nodding with him warmly. Cindy seemed flushed and aware and present. Cam looked uncomfortable, jiggling his leg and glancing between his father and the floor. Oscar continued. "I want to share with you kids something really important your mom and I discovered from that whole scary experience. We were forced to look a little more closely into how we support each other in this family. We realized that we both grew up in homes that were, through no fault of our parents, not very attentive."

When Oscar paused here, Cam looked up quickly and said, "What do you mean, Dad?" giving away that he had indeed been listening intently.

From here, they went on to have an absorbing conversation. Oscar and Olive talked about their own childhoods with their children in a candid, more vulnerable way than they had ever done before. Oscar shared more about his mother's anxiety attacks, and Olive talked about running the household and caring for her younger siblings as her single mom was keeping them afloat. They talked about how they grew up with very little awareness that what they felt, what they liked, and what they needed mattered. They talked about how they now realized that they had, despite loving Cindy and Cameron deeply, inadvertently raised them the same way.

"We went to see a therapist, and we learned all kinds of new things about relationships and what really matters, and it's changed everything for us," Olive told them.

Besides asking a few questions, Cindy and Cam didn't talk a lot during this family conversation. But they listened. They learned invaluable information about their parents and themselves, which would come up in different ways, at different times, throughout the next decade. In fact this talk, in some subtle but substantial way, was a turning point in the relationship between the four of them.

Going forward, Cindy and Cam texted more freely with each other, sharing jokes and stories between them. Cindy began sometimes calling her mother and father for advice or support. She still got frustrated with her parents sometimes, as all children do, but she seldom snapped at them out of the blue anymore. Instead, she tended to tell them exactly what she was annoyed about.

Now back to that Saturday evening after Thanksgiving, as they were walking from dessert to Cindy's apartment in Providence. Oscar and Olive held hands, walking slowly while Cindy and

Cam moved more quickly ahead of them, each glancing down at their phones, Cindy shoving Cameron off the sidewalk, and Cam attempting to trip her in return.

"Cindy, be careful! Don't push your brother into the street!" Olive called to her children. Oscar chuckled to himself at this hearkening back to when the children were small.

Then, looking up at the night sky, he breathed in the brisk November air and sighed contentedly.

"I'm the luckiest man in the world," he thought to himself.

EPILOGUE

In the acknowledgments at the beginning of this book, I mentioned seven words my father said to me as he was dying of cancer that formed the beginnings of my awareness of the power of Childhood Emotional Neglect. In fact, over time, his words have also affected me on many other levels, in some vital, unshakable way.

My dad was a born and bred farmer in the middle of the country. He worked long hours running our family farm. I have few memories of my father as I was growing up, as he always seemed to have other things on his mind than his third child. In hindsight, I think he was driven to make the farm a success. He wanted, above all else, not only to support his family, but to excel at it.

Since, to me, my dad always seemed overwhelmed and irritable, I avoided him. In my mind, this worked fine. I grew into a teenager, left the house for college, and gave him little thought. He had always provided for me materially, and for that I was deeply appreciative, but I didn't feel much else there. "I don't need anything from him," I had convinced myself. I believed that for years.

Until the day I got the call that he had been diagnosed with lung cancer.

During my trips to Oklahoma to help take care of him in the home of my brother and sister-in-law, I got to know him in a way that was very important. He asked me questions about myself and my life, and we talked about the years on the farm. Ironically, it was only now, when his time was so very limited, that we both finally found the time to communicate.

One day, about one month before he passed away, my brother and sister and our families were all there with him to celebrate Father's Day. It was a bittersweet occasion for us, as we all knew he did not have much time left.

Sitting around the living room, all of us talking and joking, my dad suddenly announced, in a way that conveyed deep conviction, *"I'm the luckiest man in the world.* I mean it. I am. The luckiest man in the world."

After a brief pause, conversation continued around him. But I was stunned. How could my father, who was in constant pain and who had so little time left to live, possibly feel that way? It took a few days of contemplation for his words to fully sink in.

Those seven words were his way of expressing what he truly felt in that moment. That the feelings he had for the people in that room—his children and their husbands and wives and his grandchildren, all whom he knew and loved so well—were the most important thing of all in this world.

In those words, I finally heard something deep and vital that would forever change my sense of myself, and plant the seeds that would ultimately result in the writing of this book.

With those words I finally understood, and truly felt, that to him, I mattered.

ABOUT THE AUTHOR

 **Jonice Webb, PhD** is a clinical psychologist and bestselling author. She is known internationally for her pioneering work in Childhood Emotional Neglect.

Throughout 20 years of practicing psychotherapy, Dr. Webb noticed a distinct cluster of symptoms among highly dissimilar clients. In searching for the common cause of this cluster of symptoms, she discovered the source: Emotional Neglect during childhood.

In 2012, Dr. Webb published the groundbreaking book, *Running on Empty: Overcome Your Childhood Emotional Neglect*, and began five years of speaking and writing about Emotional Neglect. She has been interviewed by NPR and *The Chicago Tribune*, and her work has been featured in Psychology Today, Elephant Journal and many other U.S. and international publications.

After receiving thousands of requests for help from people all over the world, Dr. Webb created Fuel Up For Life, an online recovery program for Childhood Emotional Neglect. She writes a weekly blog on the Childhood Emotional Neglect Page on PsychCentral.com.

Dr. Webb runs a private psychotherapy practice in Lexington, Massachusetts where she specializes in treating Childhood Emotional Neglect in individuals, couples and families.

She lives with her husband in the Boston area.

www.blogs.psychcentral.com/childhood-neglect
www.emotionalneglect.com
www.facebook.com/JWebbPhd
http://www.youtube.com/c/DrJoniceWebbphd
Twitter: @jwebbphd

REFERENCES

Goleman, Daniel. *Emotional Intelligence.* New York: Bantam, 2005.

Helliwell, JF and Grover, S. "How's Life at Home? New Evidence on Marriage and the Setpoint for Happiness." *The National Bureau of Economic Research.* December, 2014.

Law, Kenneth S.; Wong, Chi-Sum; Song, Lynda J. "The Construct and Criterion Validity of Emotional Intelligence and Its Potential Utility for Management Studies." Journal of Applied Psychology, Vol 89(3), Jun 2004, 483-496.

Moore, Kristin A., Kinghorn, Andrea and Bandy, Tawana. "Parental Relationship Quality and Child Outcomes Across Subgroups." Child Trends Research Brief, 2011.

Rosenberg, Ross. *The Human Magnet Syndrome.* Pesi Publishing and Media, 2013.

Sanders, CW and Sadosky, M., et al. "Learning Basic Surgical Skills with Mental Imagery: Using the Simulation Centre in the Mind." *Medical Education,* Vol 42 (2008): 607-612.

Urquijo, I., Extremera, N. and Villa A. "Emotional Intelligence, Life Satisfaction and Psychological Well-Being in Graduates: The Mediating Effect of Perceived Stress." *Applied Research in Quality of Life,* Vol 11(4), Dec 2016, 1241-1252.

U.S. Dept. of Health and Human Services. Report of the Surgeon General. *Facing Addiction in America*, 2016.

RESOURCES

Facing Your Shame and Taking Risks

Brown, Brene. *Rising Strong*. Random House Trade Paperbacks, 2017.

Improving Your Marriage

Gottman, John. *The Seven Principles for Making a Marriage Work*, Harmony, 2015.

Improving Your Relationship with a Highly Emotional Person

Kreger, Randi, *The Essential Family Guide to Borderline Personality Disorder: New Tools and Techniques to Stop Walking on Eggshells*, Hazelden Publications, 2008.

Learning More about Parenting

Faber, Adele and Mazlish, Elaine, *How to Talk So Kids Will Listen & Listen So Kids Will Talk,* Scribner, 2012.

Learning Mindfulness

HealthJourneys.com

Learning Assertiveness

Smith, Manuel J. *When I say No I Feel Guilty,* Bantam, 1975.

Improving Your Self-Esteem

McKay, Matthew and Fanning, Patrick. *Self-Esteem: A Proven Program of Cognitive Techniques for Assessing, Improving & Maintaining Your Self-Esteem,* New Harbinger, 2016.

Morgan James
Speakers Group

www.TheMorganJamesSpeakersGroup.com

We connect Morgan James published authors with live and online events and audiences who will benefit from their expertise.

www.ingramcontent.com/pod-product-compliance
Lightning Source LLC
Jackson TN
JSHW080158141224
75386JS00029B/908